CW01024558

# Creeping Fascism

Brexit, Trump and the
Rise of the Far Right

## Neil Faulkner
with Samir Dathi

publicreading
ROOMS
www.prruk.org

Published in 2017 by Public Reading Rooms
Visit our website at www.prruk.org
© Neil Faulkner
ISBN 9780995535237

*Only one thing could have stopped our movement – if our adversaries had understood its principles and from the first day had smashed, with the utmost brutality, the nucleus of our new movement.*

Adolf Hitler
1933

*So the Wolf lifted the latch, and the door flew open. And jumping without a word on the bed, he gobbled up the poor old lady. Then he put on her clothes, and tied her cap over his head, got into bed, and drew the blankets over him.*

*All this time, Red-Cap was still gathering flowers. And when she had picked as many as she could carry, she remembered her grandmother, and made haste to the cottage. She wondered very much to see the door wide open. And when she got into the room, she began to feel very ill, and exclaimed, 'How sad I feel! I wish I had not come today.'*

*Then she said, 'Good morning,' but received no answer. So she went up to the bed, and drew back the curtains, and there lay her grandmother, as she thought, with the cap drawn half over her eyes, looking very fierce.*

*'Oh, grandmother, what great ears you have!'*

*'The better to hear you with,' was the reply.*

*'And what great eyes you have!'*

*'The better to see you with.'*

*'And what great hands you have!'*

*'The better to touch you with.'*

*'But, grandmother, what great teeth you have!'*

*'The better to eat you with.' And scarcely were the words out of the mouth, when the Wolf made a spring out of bed, and swallowed up poor Little Red-Cap.*

'Little Red-Cap' (aka 'Little Red Riding-hood')
A traditional German folk-tale
The Brothers Grimm
1857

# Contents

# Introduction

This book is about one simple idea: that the wave of racism and reaction sweeping the world is the modern form of fascism.

When Britain voted for Brexit, we had a sense it was a watershed. By we, I mean myself, Samir Dathi, who worked on the book as research assistant and critic, and a small group of comrades who held broadly similar views, some of whom – Robin Beste, Andrew Burgin, Phil Hearse, Kate Hudson, and Fred Leplat – became critical readers of draft chapters as they were written.[1]

A watershed? We think so, in that it was a moment when much of the Left was suddenly overtaken by history and transformed into the wrong sort of left – the left behind, clutching an out-of-date tract. The Brexit referendum, we had realised early on, was not going to be about the fact that the EU is a bankers' consortium hardwired for austerity, privatisation, and greed: it was going to be about racism.

When we looked across Europe, moreover, we could see the pattern. It was not the Left that was going to tear the EU down to create 'Another Europe' – one of equality, democracy, peace, and sustainability: it was the Far Right. The EU was to be replaced not by socialism, but by authoritarian nationalism laced with anti-migrant and Islamophobic racism.

Then came Trump's election victory. Who could doubt it now? This, surely, was a qualitative shift in global politics? Not a gradual change, but a sudden lurch to the right, away from liberal democracy towards a police state enforcing nationalism, racism, and sexism. Towards fascism.

What we did not anticipate when we set out to write the book – at top speed, with a burning sense of urgency, even panic – was that our perspective would be confirmed by events so quickly. The Muslim ban was a terrible shock. We had never imagined that the Trump regime would move so far, so fast. Yet there it was, before the book was finished, suddenly upon us: our own *Kristallnacht*. That was the moment, in November 1938, when a vicious anti-semitic pogrom awakened the world to the enormity of what was unfolding inside Nazi Germany. Now, with the Muslim ban, the world had got the same sort of shock. It was obvious that Trump was a fascist in all but name.

That was not the only shock. When we started writing, we were quite despondent. The Left seemed so weak, divided, marginal. Resistance was minimal. We drafted the early chapters more in fear than hope: we saw a great steamroller of fascism running towards us and nothing to stop it.

Then, in the space of barely a week, two explosions of mass protest, the first in defence of women's rights, the second in solidarity with Muslims and migrants, brought millions onto the streets. We found ourselves suddenly part of a new mass movement of the Left.

What was immediately obvious was the huge gap between the Old Left and the idealistic young people on the demos. You could see it outside Downing Street on the evening of Monday 30 January at the anti-Trump protest following the ban. Whitehall was chocker. It took half an hour to squeeze your way from the middle of the crush to the edge. There must have been 50,000 people, maybe more.

The organised Left was not only swamped: it was not connecting. The slogans on the printed placards were stale. No mention of Brexit paving the road for Trump. No use of the F-word. One group was doling out a broadsheet with the 'Take Back Control' slogan of the Leave campaign as a headline.

The young people were in a different universe. A bunch of them grabbed some placards emblazoned 'Brexit, Trump, Sound the Alarm!' and started bouncing up and down in unison chanting, 'Hey, Hey, Ho, Ho, Brexit, Trump, One and the Same!' Many of the homemade placards carried the same message: 'Brexit means bowing down to bigots', 'Brexit means Trump'. Others cut to the chase: 'History is Happening Now. Resist!', 'History Will Judge Us This Day', *'No Pasaran!* 75 Years On, Still United Against Fascism', and the plain and simple 'Fuck Fascism!'

Lots of school students were there. 'I am scared by these events,' said Eli, a sixth-former from St Albans. 'I thought it couldn't happen here. I remember studying this in history.' His friend Tiggy had also been shocked into action: 'It's terrifying what they're doing. It's been a really sudden, violent change.'

Laura, an American artist living in London, was there to 'show Trump that the world rejects what he stands for', Cathrine, a graphic designer from Norway, because what was happening was 'outrageous, depressing, horrible', Grace, an American student, because 'we were supposed to be moving forwards, not backwards', and Milla, her Finnish friend, also a student, because she was 'scared about everything that is happening'.

The faces of the ethnic-minority workers in the cafés, restaurants, and junk-food joints in Leicester Square spoke a thousand words as an impromptu march passed through, roaring out the slogan 'No Hate, No Fear, Refugees are Welcome Here'. You could see the people watching lifted up. You could see it in the smiles, in the scrambles to capture the moment with a smart-phone pic to share with mates, in the reaction of the young Asian worker on the first floor of McDonald's giving the clenched-fist salute of the oppressed the world over.

Thank God! Thank someone anyway. We were on the move. This felt like the dawning of a mass anti-fascist movement. It was not all doom and gloom after all. Suddenly it seemed that we might win. Perhaps we could in fact stop them.

'Never Again!' it said on some of the cardboard placards.

'Theresa the Appeaser' it said on others.[2] The sense of history – of standing in the shadow of the 1930s – was palpable.

Adolf Hitler had become Chancellor of Germany in January 1933. It had taken time for most people to realise the significance. The Liberals voted through the emergency powers that turned Hitler into a dictator. The Social Democrats kept their heads down in the hope they might survive. The Communists announced that Hitler would not last and then it would be their turn.

Soon, most of these people were in the camps. Later, most of them would be killed. Only too late did the German Left – what little remained of it – grasp the import of what had happened.

The rest of Europe's divided Left also struggled to recognise the danger. When it did so, or enough of it did so, resistance erupted – in Vienna and Paris in 1934, in Barcelona and London in 1936.

But looking back now, we can see that by then the balance had already shifted too far; that January 1933 was the great turning-point, the fork in history's road, the moment when the world began its descent to the barbarism of Stalingrad, Auschwitz, and Hiroshima.

The historical experience is rich in lessons. Provided enough of us learn those lessons, provided enough of us understand what fascism is and how you fight it, provided enough of us organise, mobilise, and resist in ways that are effective – provided all that, we can make a reality of 'Never Again!'

This book is intended as a modest contribution to that effort – to the great historical struggle that is now upon us; a struggle to prevent the history of the 1930s repeating itself in the early 21st century; a struggle to break fascism before it breaks us, and to open the road to an alternative future and a world transformed.

In Chapter 1, we recall the double whammy of Brexit and Trump and say something about why they happened. In

Chapters 2 and 3, we use the lessons of the past to define fascism and describe how it works. Then we move to the present. Chapter 4 analyses the multi-faceted crisis of the modern capitalist system, the context for what we see as fascism's 'second wave'. Chapter 5 offers an overview of the Far Right today, drawing out the similarities and differences with interwar fascism. Chapter 6 tries to knock down the argument that what we face today is not really fascism. In Chapter 7, we discuss different ways of fighting fascism, and, on the basis of what seems to have worked in the past, we present our 'golden rules' for the anti-fascist movement. The Conclusion offers a 12-point summary of our theory of 'creeping fascism', and the Postscript brings us up to date as of the time of writing.

This, then, is a book for activists – for those already active, and those yet to become so. Because only those who are active become part of history, become makers and shakers, people who make a difference. As young Hannah, one of three school friends in Whitehall on 30 January, put it: 'You have to stand up for what is right. In the future, I want to look back and say: I was there.'

Neil Faulkner
St Albans
February 2017

# 6 Creeping Fascism

# CHAPTER 1
# Hitler's shadow?

It was one of those moments when the world changed. Like the fall of the Berlin Wall in 1989, the bombing of the Twin Towers in 2001, and the financial crash of 2008, the election of Donald Trump as US president in November 2016 sent shock-waves across the globe.

The Far Right was euphoric. Not only had the Republican Party's traditional conservatives been marginalised by the Trump campaign, but now the entire Washington political elite had been vanquished. The American liberal tradition – for which the Obama presidency had, in some sense, been an apotheosis – had suddenly collapsed. 'This is one of the most exciting nights of my life,' proclaimed former Ku Klux Klan leader David Duke. 'Make no mistake, our people have played a huge role in electing Trump!'[1]

Many of the 66 million Americans who had voted Democrat were in despair. Some had voted with enthusiasm, far more with relative indifference, even distaste; but all Clinton voters perhaps shared the sense that the alternative was a creature from the Dark Side, the political incarnation of another America, hidden until now, hideous to behold, that they did not recognise.

Commentators struggled for words. A billionaire tax-dodger, a ranting racist, a misogynist and self-confessed abuser of women, a bully who taunts the disabled and the bereaved, a serial liar, a man proud of his bigotry, his hatred, his contempt for most of humanity, this man had just been elected to the most powerful political position on the planet. Sixty-three million Americans had voted for a political psychopath.

Here, for example, is Oxford historian Jane Caplan's attempt to come to terms with the enormity of what had happened:

> For months, historians of the 20th century have been look-ing nervously at Trump and asking what tools we have to understand the man, his popular appeal, and his backers – and to measure the danger he represents. Against my better judgement, I have been spotting Mussolini in this gesture or turn of phrase, Hitler in that one. I have been watching the manipulated interactions of speaker with audience, the hyperbolic political emotions, the narcis-sistic masculinity, the unbridled threats, the conversion of facile fantasies and malignant bigotries into eternal verities, the vast, empty promises, the breath-taking lies. A whole repertoire seems to have returned us to the fascisms of interwar Europe, acted out by a man whose vanity is equalled only by his ignorance.[2]

Others, of course, revelled in his triumph. Trump, antic-ipating victory, had predicted it would be 'Brexit plus, plus, plus'. And Britain's leading Brexiteers duly hailed the out-come. After meeting the President-elect in the gold-encrusted Trump Tower in New York, UKIP leader Nigel Farage emerged to announce that:

> It was a great honour to spend time with Donald Trump. He was relaxed and full of good ideas. I'm confident he will be a good president. Mr Trump's support for the US-UK relationship is very strong. This is a man with whom we can do business.[3]

Boris Johnson, another leading Brexit campaigner who became Foreign Secretary in the new post-Brexit government, had been quick to tweet his support:

> Congratulations to Donald Trump and much looking forward to working with his administration on global stability and prosperity. I believe passionately in the importance of the UK-US relationship and am confident we can take it forward together.[4]

Johnson, a supreme opportunist who had campaigned for Brexit in the (failed) hope of making himself Tory leader, had issued a series of derogatory comments on the Trump candidature during the election campaign. Now, though, the British political elite was desperate to 'normalise' Trump. Theresa May, the new Tory Prime Minister, led the charge:

> I congratulate Donald Trump on being elected as the next President of the United States. Britain and the United States are and will remain close partners on trade, security, and defence. We have a long-standing and enduring special relationship which is built on our shared values of freedom, democracy, and enterprise, and I look forward to working with President-elect Trump to ensure that we can sustain the security and prosperity of our two nations in the future.[5]

May had been carried to the premiership on the tidal wave of racism and reaction unleashed by the British EU referendum of June 2016. Led by three right-wing politicians, Nigel Farage, Boris Johnson, and Michael Gove, the Brexiteers won 52% of the popular vote by peddling vicious anti-immigrant racism under the slogan 'Take Back Control'.

## BREXIT

The millionaire owners of the right-wing press helped broadcast the Brexit message. With three times the readership of the pro-Remain press, the *Telegraph, Mail, Express, Sun,* and *Star* spewed out a stream of reactionary propaganda that precluded any proper democratic process based on informed opinion and intelligent debate.

It was, in fact, the culmination of 15 years of gutter-press bile pumped out since Western imperialism first embarked on its self-proclaimed 'War on Terror' following the attack on the Twin Towers in 2001. The bile flowed in five main channels.

First was Islamophobic demonisation of Muslim communities and their religion as incubators of a terrorist threat lurking in the shadows at home and running amok overseas in a broad swathe from Central Asia through the Middle East to North and West Africa.

Second was anti-immigrant racism directed at the great numbers of refugees from Africa and Asia displaced by war and poverty – the result, largely, of military intervention by the Western powers, arms supplies from Western corporations, and neoliberal economic policies imposed by Western agencies.

Third was a drip-drip of insinuation that the European Union was remote, bureaucratic, unaccountable, and somehow a device controlled by foreigners for screwing the British. Now this requires a little further comment. For it is indeed the case that the EU is a bankers' and bosses' club, hardwired for austerity and privatisation, geared to hoover wealth from the bottom to the top, from working people, the poor, and public services to the rich and the corporations. But that, of course, is not the concern of the millionaire owners of the gutter press. For precisely the same could be said of Westminster and the City of London. The anti-EU propaganda of the *Mail* and the *Express* has nothing to do with the interests of ordinary people. The only question for the press lords is the degree to which the British political and corporate elite should surrender power to a wider European elite.

A fourth stream of bile was another form of anti-immigrant racism, this time directed at economic migrants from the EU (with the focus almost exclusively on people from Eastern Europe). This, of course, meant a direct challenge to one of the cardinal principles of the EU, for which free movement of people is a foundation-stone, alongside free movement of goods, services, and investment.

Finally, overlapping with the other streams, there was the right-wing media's obsession with crime, benefit fraud, and law and order. These matters are routinely 'racialised'. More often than not, the threat is from some alien 'Other' – a black man, an asylum-seeker, a terrorist cell, an East European gang, a jihadist network. A sense of social breakdown, of loss of community, of fear stalking the streets is compounded with primitive, irrational, xenophobic fear of the outsider.

The vision of Britain implicit in these arguments was the diametric opposite of the cosmopolitan, multicultural, tolerant, progressive, forward-looking attitudes of most Remain voters. It does not matter that the EU as presently constituted does not reflect the ideals of these voters: that it is, in fact, the embodiment of European corporate interests. The EU referendum was not a choice between a corporate Europe and a socialist Britain. It was a choice between two different visions, two mind-sets, two ways of thinking about social relationships.

This is revealed in the EU referendum voting patterns. Polls suggest that between two-thirds and three-quarters of the following categories of people voted Remain: students, young workers, trade union members, black people, Muslims, other ethnic minority people, Labour voters, Green voters, and nationalist (SNP, Plaid Cymru, and Sinn Fein) voters. This means that most of the more organised and class-conscious working people voted Remain, presumably, generally speaking, on a vaguely progressive, anti-racist basis.

That the argument was ideologically polarised – between reactionary and progressive voters – is apparent in opinion

surveys. The table below, based on Joseph Rowntree Foundation research, shows the proportion of people holding a specific reactionary opinion who voted Leave.[6]

| Issue | Proportion holding this view voting Leave |
|---|---|
| Immigration is bad for the economy | 90% |
| Immigration should be reduced | 88% |
| Against equal opportunities for women | 80% |
| Against equal opportunities for gay people | 79% |
| For the death penalty | 76% |
| For stiffer prison sentences | 73% |

## SOCIAL CRISIS

The attempt – by sections of the Left, much of the commen-
tariat, and politicians ranging from New Labour suits to UKIP
opportunists – to interpret the Leave vote as a 'class vote' on
the basis that it represents an anti-elite electoral revolt by the
millions 'left behind by globalisation' is misconceived.

The mistake here is to conflate the social discontent at the
base of society with its political expression. There is no question that neoliberal capitalism has created a rustbelt of closed
factories, rundown public services, dead-end estates, and great
swathes of poverty, despair, and bitterness. We are locked in a
long-term crisis of stagnation and slump, of industrial decline,
of 19th century social inequality, of grotesque greed at the top
and grinding misery at the base. This is presided over by a
political elite of smarmy, self-congratulating technocrats who
represent nothing so much as corporate power and their own
tawdry careers.

The crisis – economic, social, political – is not in question. That it can give rise to class-based movements of resistance to the system, movements with progressive potential, even a vision of the world transformed, that is not in question either. But that is the polar opposite of a reactionary electoral backlash led by right-wingers and racists. The former means a mass movement of working people based on class unity, class organisation, and class struggle. The latter is the raw material of fascism.

Let us spell out the basic underlying mistake here: it is to assume that any crisis – and any outbreak of mass discontent – must somehow benefit the Left. But this is not the case. A protracted crisis makes the existing set-up increasingly intolerable. When things go wrong, when lives fall apart, people demand answers, alternatives, action; and they turn away from an old political order that cannot supply them.

In any such crisis, two parties arise to offer a way forward. One is the party of revolutionary hope (the socialists). The key message here is that united mass action from below can overturn the old order and create a new one based on democracy, equality, peace, and sustainability.

But there is also the party of counter-revolutionary despair (the fascists). Their message is that the race, the nation, the *Volk* – rich and poor, capitalist and worker, landlord and tenant – should unite against the outsider, the foreigner, the alien. Theirs is a message of division, hate, and unreason, a message which protects the elite and the system from the anger of the people by redirecting it against the oppressed.

To be able to distinguish between these two parties is, for the Left in a period of capitalist crisis, a matter of life and death.

If the monster of nationalism and racism incubating inside the Brexit camp was less than wholly apparent during the campaign, it is undeniable now. To argue that because many working-class communities voted heavily for Brexit, we are witness to some sort of popular revolt against austerity and inequality is crass stupidity. It is to make a nonsense of any distinction between the mere fact of class position – a matter of sociological description – and conscious mass struggle by working people acting for themselves to change the world.

Indeed, in some sense, the whole of socialist activity can be accounted for by this distinction. Activists want to mobilise working people in mass, democratic, class-conscious movements for change. For socialists to pretend that millions of working people voting for Farage, Johnson, and Gove – who conducted the most racist election campaign in recent British history – can somehow be interpreted as a 'class vote' or a 'left-wing victory' beggars belief.

In a crisis, the Centre cannot hold, and popular discontent can be captured and channelled by the Right or by the Left. The Left has no hope if it cannot even tell the difference. This is so important that the basic argument bears further emphasis.

The Brexit campaign was an anti-EU, anti-Westminster, anti-Establishment campaign – just as Hitler's campaign was anti-Weimar in 1932. The Brexit campaign drew upon great pools of bitterness among those at the bottom of society, the victims of globalisation, neoliberalism, and austerity – just as Hitler was supported by the unemployed, the unorganised workers, the broken small businesses, the 'little people' who felt forgotten, ignored, and abused. And the Brexit campaign fanned a great upsurge of anti-immigrant racism – just as Hitler blamed the Jews.

It could not be more straightforward. The point is well made by the authors of the Joseph Rowntree Foundation report quoted above:

> The more disadvantaged voters that turned out for Brexit are...united by values that encourage support for more socially conservative, authoritarian, and nativist responses. On the whole, Leave voters have far more in common with each other than they have things that divide them. Over three-quarters of Leave voters feel disillusioned with politicians; two-thirds support the death

penalty; and well over half feel very strongly English. Over one-third of Leave voters hold all three of these attitudes, compared to just 6% who do not hold any of them. This more liberal group of Brexit voters, therefore, constituted a very small part of the coalition for leaving the EU.[7]

In other words, the much-vaunted 'Lexit' argument – that Brexit is a class-based anti-elite revolt – revolves around the barely one in 20 Leave voters who might be considered to have consistently progressive politics. What seems incontrovertible is that the overwhelming majority of ordinary British voters with broadly liberal or left-leaning opinions voted Remain.

Leon Trotsky, the radical thinker who pioneered the Marxist analysis of fascism in the interwar years, would almost certainly have shared the Remain instinct. He argued in the mid 1920s that a 'United States of Europe' would be a progressive development, since it would be an antidote to nationalism and would expand 'the union of the workers'.

If the capitalist states of Europe succeeded in merging into an imperialist trust, this would be a step forward as compared with the existing situation, for it would first of all create a unified, all-European material base for the working class movement. The proletariat would in this case have to fight not for the return to 'autonomous' national states, but for the conversion of the imperial state trust into a European Republican Federation.[8]

## SCAGEGOATS

**SCAPEGOATS**

It may be worth reminding ourselves how racism works. It is endemic in class societies where people are forced to compete for jobs, homes, services, and so on. It reflects the fragmentation of the working class along racial, national, ethnic, and religious lines. It is a device which can be used by the ruling class to divide working people and redirect anger against the system into attacks on the oppressed.

Historically, upsurges of racism have often occurred when the system is in crisis, discontent is building, and established elites are discredited. The historical function of racism is then twofold: a) to undermine solidarity and unity in struggle; and b) to bind workers politically to ruling-class factions. That is, racism functions to frustrate collective action and reconfigure the relationship between workers and rulers. It is an alternative to the working class acting for itself and becoming an independent agent of self-emancipation.

Were it the case that the European working-class was engaged in mass struggles with the potential to bring down the state and end the rule of European finance-capital, then socialists would be right to favour the breakup of the EU in its present form, because then the alternative would be 'Another Europe' – one based, as we suggested above, on democracy, equality, peace, and sustainability. But the attack on the EU today is from the Right, not the Left, and this is always the decisive consideration in politics, because this determines which class benefits.

The British referendum was a perfect illustration of the problem. Some on the Left argued for 'Lexit' – Left Exit. Many of the same now argue for 'People's Brexit' – a British withdrawal from the EU that will somehow be anti-austerity, anti-privatisation, and anti-corporate.

The Lexit voice – the socialist case for voting Leave – was, of course, drowned in the tidal wave of nationalism and racism. The impact on voters of the broadsheets and websites of Britain's small, divided, fractious Left was virtually zero. The Leave campaign was dominated by the Brexit arguments of the millionaires, not the Lexit arguments of tiny Trotskyist groups.

These Brexit arguments – the arguments of the Far Right – were not just projected through the organs of the gutter press: they were amplified by the whole of the mainstream media.

Take the BBC, the state-controlled broadcaster. Its news coverage – already squeezed by an ever-growing torrent of

trivia about royals, celebrities, and sport – has become dominated by stories about migration, terrorism, and crime. Even
when real news is reported, the information supplied is shallow and distorted, and no connections are made between
events, as if contemporary history were simply a random
jumble of disasters, of 'one damn thing after another', without
pattern or purpose.

The Brexit disinformation campaign – and to an even
greater extent the Trump disinformation campaign in the
States – was further amplified by the 'fake news' and 'post-fact'
output of online media. In cyberspace, news has been diced
and spliced to create bespoke packages tailored to the interests and prejudices of internet users – the very negation of the
concept of news as a flow of accurate, comprehensive, objective
information about important events. Cyberspace has become
an Orwellian world of disinformation, where, each day, random
fragments of 'non-news' – artefacts of distortion, falsification,
and decontextualisation – receive millions of hits.

Thus, in a bubble of ignorance, prejudice, and lies, swelling
across a decade and a half, was the Brexit campaign's narrow
majority accumulated. Consider this selection of front-page
headlines to get a flavour:

MIGRANTS SEND OUR CRIME RATES SOARING
Police chief blames 35% rise in violence on new arrivals
*Daily Express*, 28 January 2008

THEY'VE STOLEN *ALL* OUR JOBS
1.3 M migrants took *every* Brit vacancy since 2001
*Daily Star*, 16 December 2008

GET BRITAIN OUT OF EUROPE
We want our country back
*Daily Express*, 25 November 2010

EU WANTS MIGRANTS TO TAKE OUR JOBS
*Daily Express*, 15 November 2012

MIGRANT'S MILKING BRITAIN'S BENEFITS
Foreigners more likely to claim handouts
*Daily Express*, 21 July 2015

Borders Chaos
1 M MIGRANTS HEADING THIS WAY
(and we took 558,000 last year)
*The Sun*, 22 September 2015

1 IN 5 BRIT MUSLIMS' SYMPATHY FOR JIHADIS
*The Sun*, 23 November 2015

WHO *WILL* SPEAK FOR ENGLAND?
*Daily Mail*, 4 February 2016

BELEAVE IN BRITAIN
*The Sun*, 13 June 2016

As politicians squabble over border controls, yet another
lorry load of migrants arrives in UK declaring...
WE'RE FROM EUROPE – LET US IN!
*Daily Mail*, 16 June 2016

PM knew FOUR years ago he'd never meet immigration
target while inside EU, reveals former closest aide
CAMERON'S MIGRATION DECEPTION
*Daily Mail*, 21 June 2016

Lies. Greedy elites. Or a great future outside a broken,
dying Europe...
IF YOU BELIEVE IN BRITAIN, VOTE LEAVE
*Daily Mail*, 22 June 2016

Your country needs you
VOTE LEAVE TODAY
*Daily Express*, 23 June 2016

The deeply reactionary character of the Brexit vote was well understood by UKIP leader Paul Nuttall, who proclaimed, 'My ambition is not insignificant: I want to replace the Labour Party and make UKIP the patriotic voice of working people.'

Nuttall, a state-educated northerner whose image could hardly be more different from that of the millionaire toff he replaced, plans to focus UKIP's efforts on collapsing Labour's core vote in its rustbelt heartlands. As *The Guardian* reports:

> His line of attack is already clear: that Jeremy Corbyn is an out-of-touch metropolitan figure obsessed with Palestine, fair trade, and climate change. In contrast, Nuttall will talk relentlessly about standing up for the English, putting the 'great' back into Britain, while claiming to have the solutions to 'the issues that affect real people in real working-class communities.[9]

## EURO-RACISTS

The Brexit vote and the Trump election resonated across Europe. Far-right leaders celebrated the results and predicted that it would be their turn next.

Norbert Hofer, leader of Austria's Freedom Party, an organisation founded by former SS officers that wants stronger borders, reduced benefits for immigrants, and job discrimination in favour of Austrians, hailed Trump's victory. 'Whenever the elites distance themselves from voters,' he announced, 'those elites will be voted out of office.'[10] In the event, Hofer won a similar share of the vote to Trump (46%), but failed to secure the Presidency in an election held in December 2016.

Matteo Renzi, the Italian Prime Minister, was defeated in a constitutional referendum in the same month, securing only 41% of the vote – brought down by a wave of anti-establishment sentiment fanned by the far-right Northern League and the rightward-moving Five Star Movement. As *The Independent* explained in an article that referred explicitly to 'the Trump effect':

> The Five Star Movement has crowed Donald Trump's election as evidence of a protest movement sweeping the West. It is calling on Italians to seize the opportunity of the referendum to join in.[11]

Attention is currently (as we write) focused on Holland and France. The Dutch go to the polls in a general election in March, and Geert Wilders' Freedom Party is currently front-runner, with 24% support. Wilders plans to put migration and 'Islamisation' at the heart of the party's campaign. Draft manifesto pledges include the closure of every mosque in Holland and the banning of the Koran from public buildings. 'The Netherlands have become a sick country,' Wilders told the judge when on trial for a televised speech abusing Dutch Moroccans. 'The Dutch want their country back.'

Wilders pulled ahead of his leading rival in the polls in the immediate wake of Trump's victory in the US.[12] He proclaimed the result of the US Presidential election to be a 'historic victory', a 'revolution', and the harbinger of a 'Patriotic Spring' in Europe:

> America regained its national sovereignty, its identity. It reclaimed its own democracy. That's why I called it a 'revolution'. I think that the people of America, as in Europe, feel insulted by all the politicians that ignore the real problems. We will see also in Europe that things will change, politics will never be the same

and what I call the Patriotic Spring will have an enormous incentive. The lesson for Europeans is look at America. What America can do, we can do as well.[13]

National Front leader Marine Le Pen has echoed these sentiments, declaring the Brexit and Trump votes to herald a 'worldwide movement' against 'unchecked globalisation, destructive ultra-liberalism, the elimination of nation-states, [and] the disappearance of borders' – a movement that might propel her to the French presidency in elections scheduled for April/May.[14]

Le Pen has attempted to 'de-demonise' the National Front, cleansing its appearance of fascist trappings, but it remains a deeply racist party, with entrenched local bases, like that of Mayor Robert Méynard, whose attempt to set up a militia of former soldiers and police to patrol the streets had to be blocked by the judiciary.[15]

The National Front has pulled the whole of French politics sharply to the right. At one point, it seemed the presidential run-off might see Le Pen pitted against a far-right traditional conservative peddling the same racism.

François Fillon is a Catholic social reactionary, an admirer of Margaret Thatcher, and author of a book about 'Islamic totalitarianism'. He is a fountain of coded Islamophobic racism, claiming that the country is involved in an 'ideological struggle', that 'French values' are threatened, that France is 'not a multicultural nation', that 'radical Islam is corrupting some of our Muslim fellow citizens', and that 'when you come to someone's house, by courtesy, you don't take over'.[16]

An electoral contest between Le Pen and Fillon would have been a carnival of racism and reaction – only Fillon's campaign seems to have imploded in a corruption scandal, making it more likely, at the time of writing, that Le Pen will face a neoliberal Blair clone, Emmanuel Macron, instead.

Across much of the rest of Europe, far-right and fascist

parties are advancing. Far-right authoritarian regimes hold power in Hungary and Poland. In a clutch of other European countries, similar parties enjoy the support of one in five, one in four, even one in three voters. In many places, unequivocally fascist parties – like Hungary's Jobbik, Bulgaria's Patriotic Front, Greece's Golden Dawn, and Sweden's Democrats – enjoy mass electoral support. A string of major cities have seen racist mobilisations of tens of thousands, sometimes involving disciplined paramilitary contingents, often culminating in violent attacks on minority groups, especially Muslims, Roma, and migrant communities.

The dominant image remains that of bullies in suits rather than thugs in uniform. National flags are usually preferred over fascist symbols. The talk is more often of 'our values' than of 'inferior peoples'. The message is more likely to be communicated in toxic tweets than military-style parades.

So are they in fact fascists?

It is the argument of this book that, to all intents and purposes, they are, and that we face a clear and present danger of 'creeping fascism'; that the film of the 1930s is running in slow motion; that we have begun a journey, and that if we continue on the same road, our destination could be something akin to Auschwitz.

But it is also part of our argument that fascism is a process, not a finished form, and that, while the modern Far Right is capable of evolving into the most extreme forms of fascism, it has not done so yet. This means that it is not too late; that if the Left unites, organises, and fights back, we can still block the fascist road and map out an alternative future; that we could lead humanity in another direction, towards the overthrow of finance-capital, the dispossession of the 1%, and a world transformed by mass democratic action from below.

First, though, we must arm ourselves with understanding, and to do this, we must draw on the rich historical experience of the working-class movement. We have faced fascism before, above all in the struggles of the 1930s. To the lessons of the past, therefore, we turn in the next two chapters.

The first attempts a theoretical answer, based on historical experience, to the question 'What is fascism?'. The second explores several concrete historical examples of fascism in action.

## CHAPTER 2
# What is fascism?

The term 'fascism' conjures images of massed ranks of uniformed men and a sea of swastika banners at the Nuremberg Rally in 1938. Or of smashed windows, racist graffiti, and strutting Brownshirts during the *Kristallnacht* anti-semitic pogrom that same year. Or of grainy photographs of murderers in greatcoats and jackboots toppling victims into mass graves with a bullet through the head in some nameless place in the vastness of Eastern Europe in 1941 or 1942. Or of heaps of corpses, each a jumble of rags, limbs, emaciated torsos, and lolling skulls, at the newly liberated concentration camp of Bergen-Belsen in 1945.

But mass historical phenomena like fascism cannot be defined by their most extreme expression. Not only was the German Nazi Party the most radical of the interwar fascist parties – a reflection of the depth of the country's economic, social, and political crisis in 1932 – but the Nazi regime proved to be the one that carried fascist radicalisation to its furthest limit between 1933 and 1945. The outbreak of war, the conquest of Eastern Europe, and Nazi control over tens of millions of subjugated people created the context for this radicalisation.

The demand was for 'living space' for German settlers, and therefore for what we would now call 'ethnic cleansing'. The demand was for a 'final solution' to the problem of 'racial contamination'. And the exigencies of war in occupied territories allowed work to be done in secret, beyond the range of public scrutiny, outside any framework of civilised norms. So it was here, in occupied Poland and European Russia, a full eight years after Hitler came to power, in a dark netherworld ruled by Nazi gauleiters and SS police, that the racial fantasies of fascism achieved their ultimate consummation in industrialised genocide.

We cannot answer the question 'What is fascism?' by reference to the outer limits of its barbarism. Like other political '-isms' – like monarchism, conservatism, liberalism, and socialism – it is both varied in practice, taking on a diversity of forms, and also changeable over time, having a different character at successive stages in its historical life-cycle. Fascism is not a *thing* – fixed, static, closely defined. It is a *process* – a motion, a living, growing, evolving mass movement that exists in a specific historic context and is shaped by its interactions with other social and political forces.[1]

The Nazi Holocaust represents one extreme on the spectrum, where a bureaucratised fascist state-apparatus was able to implement its 'final solution' – even though the diversion of resources and waste of labour-power was, from the point of view of Germany's traditional elite, engaged at the time in an all-out imperialist war, wholly counter-productive. But at the other extreme, fascism merges into other forms of elite rule – into, for example, straightforward military authoritarianism. Here, for example, is how Leon Trotsky, the exiled Russian revolutionary thinker, discussed the matter in relation to the authoritarian-populist regime of Joseph Pilsudski in interwar Poland:

> It is methodologically false to form an image of some 'ideal' fascism and to oppose it to this real fascist regime which has grown up, with all its peculiarities and contradictions, upon the terrain of the relationship of classes and nationalities in the Polish state. Will Pilsudski be able to lead the action of destruction of the working-class organisations to the very end? The logic of the situation

drives him inevitably on this path. That does not depend upon the formal definition of 'fascism as such', but upon the true relationship of forces, the dynamics of the political processes taking place in the masses, the strategy of the working-class vanguard, and finally, the course of events in Western Europe...[2]

Nationalist Spain between 1936 and 1939 provides another example of the wide range of fascist forms in the historical record.

The Spanish generals launched a military coup in July 1936 to overthrow the democratically elected 'Popular Front' government of liberals, socialists, and communists. The coup triggered a working-class revolution. The result was a three-year war between (right-wing) Nationalists and (left-wing) Republicans.

The Nationalist movement remained firmly under the control of the generals, but it was an alliance that included monarchists, traditional conservatives, the Catholic Church, and the Falange, a Spanish fascist movement founded by one José Antonio Primo de Rivera.

The Falange was a mass organisation which grew at tremendous speed during the war, having 75,000 members in July 1936, but nearly a million by the end of that year, an estimated 80,000 of whom were under arms. Yet it remained subordinate to the Spanish military. Nonetheless, the main consequence of the Nationalist victory – the destruction of the Left, the labour movement, and liberal parliamentary democracy – was precisely the same as that of the Nazi seizure of power in Germany. And so were the methods: at least 200,000 people – perhaps twice that number – were murdered during and in the immediate aftermath of the Civil War.[3]

Further complication arises from the way in which fascist movements evolved over time. In the view of Robert Paxton, a leading academic authority, we can identify five stages in the historical development of a successful fascist movement: formation; growth inside the political system; seizure of power;

exercise of power; and 'the long duration', when, over time, the regime may either radicalise or deflate into a more routine form of authoritarian rule.[4]

We seem to be no nearer an overarching definition. Fascism becomes a slippery concept, the meaning running between our fingers; whatever it is seems so varied and changeable that we cannot get a grip on it. The temptation is to give up and perhaps regard definition as a pointless exercise in semantics.

But we cannot: because if we do not understand a political threat, if we do not have a clear view of what it is we face, we cannot possibly develop appropriate strategies for combating it. And history leaves us in no doubt that fascism is a mortal threat to personal freedom, civil and political rights, social reform and progressive change, and, in the long run, any attempt to build a movement to fight for radical transformation in the interests of ordinary working people. The lesson of history is that fascism can lead to the barbarism of war, ethnic cleansing, and industrialised genocide.

So we must stick with our question: 'What is fascism?'

## THE CONTEXT

'The truth is the whole' wrote the great German philosopher Georg Hegel. That is: to understand any part of social reality, we must understand the whole of it, for everything is interacting with and being shaped by everything else. Nothing is entire unto itself – all things are dependent and contingent.

Sadly, this insight of early 19th century German thought is rarely heeded in either academic or political discourse. Many attempts to define fascism fail for this reason: they attempt to identify one or two 'essential' characteristics – a middle-class mass base, for example, or the existence of uniformed paramilitaries, or the failure of a liberal political regime, or an unresolved conflict between 'tradition' and 'modernity', or whatever – instead of beginning their analysis with an understanding of the 'conjuncture' as a whole.

We are going to introduce some technical terms, because we think we need them. 'Conjuncture' is one of them. By conjuncture – or state of affairs – we mean a specific moment in historical time and geographical space which constitutes the framework for contemporary economic, social, political, and cultural events. Each conjuncture is unique. History repeats itself, but never exactly. We can draw lessons from the past, but the future remains an unexplored continent.

You sometimes hear people say 'History keeps on repeating itself, and we never learn from it'. You also hear people say 'We don't need history and theories. We shouldn't lecture people as if we know better. We should listen and learn from their experience.'

We feel very strongly that all these ideas are misconceived. We are firm believers in Marxist theory, which we see as the accumulated, concentrated, synthesised experience of the struggles of millions of working people over some two centuries. We would argue: a) that we can learn from this experience; and b) that not to do so is irresponsible. Politics is not a hobby. Socialists have an obligation to educate themselves so that they can act effectively to change the world.

So we take theory seriously. We study history – our history, the people's history – because we can distill from it theoretical lessons which should enable us to fight better, with a greater chance of victory for our side, in the future. Ignorance never helped anyone, so let us not pretend it is a virtue.

We need theory to understand the conjuncture; to understand the conjuncture is to understand the whole; and understanding the whole is the starting-point for understanding a social movement like fascism.

In 'normal' times, fascism is restricted to a fringe of political crackpots with minimal influence. It is only in periods of crisis that it has the capacity to become a mass phenomenon. The interwar years were such a period of crisis.

The world economy never recovered from the unravelling of the war economies of 1914-18. Massive cuts in arms

expenditure reduced demand. This resulted in a self-perpetuating cycle of falling output, falling profits, and falling wages.
Growth rates remained well below those of the years before
and during the war. Unemployment shot up after 1918 and
stayed high for the next two decades.

With demand in the 'real economy' depressed, capital
flowed into debt and speculation, creating a bubble economy
of inflated asset prices and 'get-rich-quick' schemes – the
world of the 'Roaring Twenties' satirised in Scott Fitzgerald's
*The Great Gatsby*.

When the bubble burst – spectacularly, in the Wall Street
Crash of 1929 – the world economy was plunged deeper into
depression. As demand collapsed, austerity governments across
the world made cuts 'to balance the budget' (and safeguard the
wealth of the rich), driving the economy ever downwards, until,
by 1932, one in four was out of work in Germany and the United
States, the two biggest economies.

This was the 'Great Depression', the 'Hungry Thirties' – the
period depicted in John Steinbeck's *The Grapes of Wrath* – a
period of permanent mass unemployment, of wage cuts and
desperate poverty, of farm closures and forced migration, of
lives collapsing and communities breaking apart.

The war and the post-war economic depression – carnage
followed by poverty – had powered a great wave of revolutionary struggle across the world between 1917 and 1923. Fascism
first emerged as a mass force in this period. It was a reaction
to – and the polar opposite of – the revolutionary movement
represented by the unions, the left parties, and the democratic
mass assemblies.

The political situation stabilised in the mid 1920s. The
economy recovered a little, the radical tide receded, and the fascists shrank back to the fringe of political life – except in Italy,
where they had broken through and come to power.

But a huge labour movement with a tradition of militant
struggle had been created, and when the economy nosedived

after 1929, support for the Far Left surged again. In February 1934, for example, the workers of Paris were mobilised in huge union-organised demonstrations against fascism, and the workers of Vienna mounted a four-day insurrection against the far-right regime of Engelbert Dolfuss. In May-June 1936, the industrial struggle in France swelled into a massive general strike and a wave of factory occupations, and the following month, July 1936, the Spanish working class rose in revolt against a military coup backed by the fascists, taking control of half the country. This second surge of the interwar European class struggle peaked in the city of Barcelona in 1936-37.[5] The English socialist and writer George Orwell was a witness:

> It was the first time that I had ever been in a town where the working class was in the saddle. Practically every building had been seized by the workers and was draped with red flags or with the red-and-black flags of the anarchists...
>
> Every shop and café had an inscription saying that it had been collectivised; even the bootblacks had been collectivised and their boxes painted red and black. Waiters and shop-workers looked you in the face and treated you as an equal. Servile and even ceremonial forms of speech had temporarily disappeared...
>
> There were no private motor-cars, they had all been commandeered, and all the trams and taxis and much of the other transport was painted red and black. The revolutionary posters were everywhere, flaming from the walls in clean reds and blues that made the few remaining advertisements look like daubs of mud...
>
> And it was the aspect of the crowds that was the queerest thing of all. In outward appearance, it was a town in which the wealthy classes had practically ceased to exist... Practically everyone wore rough working-class clothes, or blue overalls, or some variant

of the militia uniform...

Above all, there was a belief in the revolution and the future, a feeling of having suddenly emerged into an era of equality and freedom. Human beings were trying to behave as human beings and not as cogs in the capitalist machine.[6]

The working people of Barcelona had turned their world upside down. They had stormed the heavens, toppled the rich, and were building a new society from the bottom up. They were the worst nightmares of every banker in Europe made flesh and blood. The possibility they represented – of socialist revolution – was an essential part of the wider context for fascism.

The European workers' movement of the interwar period constituted a mortal threat to the capitalist system and the wealth and power of traditional elites. The Russian Revolution had shown that the old order could be crumbled to dust. Economic crisis and social discontent kept the continent on edge for the next two decades. Successive explosions of class revolt in a string of major cities showed that the threat had not been extinguished.

Fascism was a direct response to that threat: it was a mass movement of the Right – that is, a mass *counter-revolutionary* movement – that grew during the interwar period in reaction to the revolutionary potential of the working class.

## CORPORATE POWER:
## THE ECONOMICS OF FASCISM

Photomontage artist John Heartfield, who worked on behalf of the German Communist Party in the 1930s, published an image entitled *The meaning of the Hitler salute: little man asks for big gifts*. It showed a diminutive Hitler receiving funds in his upraised palm from a much larger figure, representing big business, standing immediately behind him. Another Heartfield image that year, entitled *Adolf, the superman, swallows gold and spouts tin*, shows Hitler making a speech, but in the X-ray view of his torso we see a swastika over his heart and a pile of gold in the pit of his stomach.[7]

Heartfield's message – that fascism was a façade and corporate power the substance – echoed that of the world communist movement at the time. This message contained an essential truth, but it was also an oversimplification, and crude versions of the argument implied that Hitler was simply a puppet of the bosses, as if a complex social phenomenon like fascism could be reduced to mere masquerade.

The appeal of such arguments – variants of conspiracy theory – is that they are simple and easy to grasp: the stuff of slogans and sound-bites. But all conspiracy theories are false in so far as they focus on one aspect of social reality and ignore the wider context (remember that: 'the truth is the whole'). Nonetheless, Heartfield's images do capture *part* of the reality.

Some bosses were certainly very sympathetic to fascism in the interwar period. Between 1920 and 1922, US car manufacturer Henry Ford published a series of anti-semitic essays in a newspaper he owned, *The Dearborn Independent*, and then turned these into a four-volume book entitled *The International Jew*, which was later republished by the Ku Klux Klan and, in German translation, by the Nazis.[8] The Italian Fascist Party was in receipt of business donations from 1919 onwards, and in the crucial political crisis of autumn 1922, leading Milan industrialists, including Giovanni Pirelli and Camillo Olivetti, urged the Italian Prime Minister to bring Mussolini into a government coalition.[9] The coal and steel magnate Fritz Thyssen was a long-standing supporter of Hitler, providing funds as early as 1923, and he was joined by many other leading German capitalists after the 1929 Crash.[10] Lord Rothermere, owner of *The Daily Mail*, financed Oswald Mosley's British Union of Fascists in 1934, and helped broadcast its message, most notoriously with his *Hurrah for the Blackshirts!* article.[11]

Nonetheless, big-business support for fascism tended to be limited until the movement was very strong. At that point, however, traditional elites might play a decisive role in elevating fascists to power. Sometimes, as in Spain, where the generals remained in control of the far-right movement, the fascists played a subordinate role. But in two cases – in Italy in 1922 and Germany in 1933 – they achieved state power in their own right.

Mussolini's 'March on Rome' could have been stopped by the Italian state: the army and the police, had they been ordered into action, could have dispersed the fascist bands with ease. Instead, King Victor Emmanuel, backed by many Italian landowners and industrialists, appointed Mussolini prime minister.

In Germany, the Nazis' spectacular electoral advance went into reverse in the course of 1932, their vote falling from 37% in July to 33% in November. So Hitler did not come to power through electoral victory. Nor did he 'seize' power by armed force. He was elevated to power by President Paul von Hindenburg, Germany's celebrated field-marshal, in what was effectively a palace coup, though with the support of a substantial fraction of the country's economic, political, and military leadership. This, as Hitler biographer Ian Kershaw remarks, was 'a drama that unfolded largely out of sight of the German people'.[12]

Fascists have never, in fact, battered their way to power in a coup directed against traditional elites and the existing state-apparatus. To advance beyond a certain point, they have invariably had to cut deals with the system, and the closer they have come to power, the greater has been their inclination to rein back on anti-elite rhetoric and street violence so as to appear 'respectable' and 'safe'.

Here we arrive at a critical part of our definition. Whatever the rhetoric, fascism in practice is neither anti-elite nor anti-system: it is a defensive bulwark of capital and the state against a potentially insurgent working class.

'Should fascism come to power,' Trotsky warned the German Communists, 'it will ride over your skulls and spines like a terrific tank.'[13] So it was. Once in power, the Nazis were ruthlessly pro-business. Democracy was dismantled. Trade

unions and the left parties were smashed. Activists were
rounded up, imprisoned, sometimes murdered. The working-
class movement was decapitated and pulverised. Work rates
increased and wages were depressed. Between 1932 and
1939, the profits of AEG, Siemens, and I G Farben doubled,
those of BMW and Krupp tripled.[14]

Soaring profits reflected not only the smashing of labour
organisation, but also a major expansion of the German economy after 1933. That Nazi policy was *rational* from the point
of view of major German corporations must be stressed. In
contrast to most governments at the time, which were actively
*deflating* their economies – and thereby deepening the depression by sucking demand out of the system – Nazi policy was
*reflationary*.

The aim was 'autarchy' – national self-sufficiency – through
the construction of an independent economic bloc insulated
from the vagaries of world trade (the opposite of 'globalisation'). To achieve this, the state had to become a major economic actor (so another term for this sort of approach might be
'state capitalism'). State intervention took various forms: pro-
tectionist tariffs, capital controls, and currency management to
control inflows of foreign goods and stem outflows of domestic
capital; deficit spending to fund infrastructure projects, mop
up unemployment, and inject demand into the economy; and
state contracts to private capital, especially heavy industries,
construction firms, and arms manufacturers.

The effect was to lift the German economy out of the
depression with a strong dose of 'Keynesian' demand stimulus.
Modest amounts of state spending soon triggered a 'multiplier
effect', whereby firms which secured state contracts, and the
workers they employed, generated demand for other goods,
which in turn generated demand for yet more goods, giving rise
to a self-feeding economic boom.

In other circumstances, with unemployment falling dra-
matically, workers might have gone onto the offensive to secure

higher wages. But the unions had been smashed and replaced by a compulsory 'Labour Front' which enshrined the subordination of labour to capital in a new 'corporate state'. The first clause of the labour law stated:

> In each establishment, the owner of the undertaking as the leader of the establishment and the salaried and wage-earning employees as his followers shall work together for the furtherance of the purposes of the establishment and for the benefit of the nation and the state in general.[15]

Nazi rule, in other words, meant bosses' power. Robert Ley, the leader of the Labour Front, was quite explicit about this:

> The building up of the corporate state will, as a first thing, restore to the natural leader of the enterprise, to the employer, the complete management and thereby also the responsibility. The factory council consists of workers, employees, and employer. Nevertheless, it has only an advisory vote. The decision rests with the employer alone.[16]

This programme of political economy – a corporate state running a national-capitalist bloc – meant a sharp turning-away from free trade and globalisation. But rapid economic growth merely increased the demand for raw materials and the need for markets. Oswald Mosley, the British fascist leader in the 1930s, saw the British Empire – 'within whose borders can be found nearly every resource, human and material, which industry requires' – as the solution.[17] Hitler's problem was that Germany was a continental power without an empire, such that the development of a viable autarchic bloc required, at least in the long run, imperial expansion.

Nazi militarism and aggression, therefore, was not an aberration: it reflected the interests of German capital. The Treaty of

Versailles (at the end of the First World War) had stripped away much of Germany's territory, built up rival states on its borders, and imposed crippling reparations and arms limitations. This was bad enough: but the collapse of world trade in the 1930s meant that Germany's economic recovery was at risk of being choked by lack of raw materials and closed markets.

In short, continuing capital accumulation could not be accommodated within existing national boundaries. Germany needed the ironworks of Alsace-Lorraine, the arms industries of Czechoslovakia, the coalmines of Poland, and the oilfields of Romania; perhaps even the grain-producing regions of the Ukraine and the oilfields of the distant Caucasus or Middle East.[18]

Nazi imperialism was not the posturing of some deranged despot intent upon 'world domination'. Hitler's demands for *Lebensraum* ('living space') at the expense of Slavic *Untermenschen* ('sub-humans') expressed – albeit in grotesquely racialised language – German capitalism's drive for empire in Central and Eastern Europe.

So fascism smashed democracy and the labour movement, rebuilt the economy, boosted profits, and prepared for imperialist war. It was counter-revolutionary, pro-capitalist, and pro-state. For these reasons, it was backed by traditional elites after the existing system – liberal parliamentary democracy – broke down in the crisis of the interwar period.

As Trotsky described the Nazi 'seizure' of power: 'Bourgeois democracy transforms itself legally, pacifically, into a fascist dictatorship. The secret is simple enough: bourgeois democracy and fascist dictatorship are the instruments of one and the same class, the exploiters.'[19] The transition, he explained, had been made necessary by the fact that democracy had collapsed under the pressures of the crisis.[20]

The historic role of fascism – to save the system in a crisis – is now clear. But a question remains. What distinguishes it from mere dictatorship; from, say, a junta of generals? The answer, of course, is the mass movement. Fascism may or may not result in an assumption of state power and the creation of a totalitarian dictatorship. But it is always an attempt to build a mass movement. To this we now turn.

## HUMAN DUST: THE SOCIOLOGY OF FASCISM

The interwar fascist mass movements struck critical observers as an eruption from the social depths, an upsurge of unreason, a 'return of the repressed', a reversion to a primeval barbarism. Whence this madness? From what deranged social material was fascism constructed?

'Through the fascist agency,' Trotsky argued,

> capitalism sets in motion the masses of the crazed petty-bourgeoisie, and bands of the declassed and demoralised lumpenproletariat; all the countless human-beings whom finance-capital itself has brought to desperation and frenzy. From fascism, the bourgeoisie demands a thorough job; once it has resorted to methods of civil war, it insists on having peace for a period of years. And the fascist agency, by utilising the petty-bourgeoisie as a battering-ram, by overwhelming all obstacles in its path, does a thorough job.
>
> After fascism is victorious, finance-capital gathers into its hands, as in a vice of steel, directly and immediately, all the organs and institutions of sovereignty, the executive, administrative, and educational powers of the state: the entire state-apparatus together with the army, the municipalities, the universities, the schools, the press, the trade unions, and the co-operatives.
>
> When a state turns fascist, it does not only mean that the forms and methods of government are changed... but it means, primarily and above all, that the workers' organisations are annihilated; that the working class is reduced to an amorphous state; and that a system of administration is created which penetrates deeply into

the masses and which serves to frustrate the independent crystallisation of the working class. Therein precisely is the gist of fascism.[21]

What is the argument here? That fascism is an instrument of the 'bourgeoisie' – the capitalist class, the corporate elite, the 1%. That the mass movement is formed primarily of the 'petty-bourgeoisie' – the middle class – and to a lesser extent of the 'lumpenproletariat' – the most depressed and demoralised section of the working class. And that this movement is used to propel the fascists to power, to shatter working-class organisation, and thus to secure the rule of capital.

The nuances in this conception of fascism have been much debated. Some have stressed the role of big business, arguing, in a somewhat crude and mechanical way, that fascism can be reduced to a mere expression of *capitalist* interests. Some have emphasised the other side of Trotsky's equation, stressing fascism's fundamentally *middle class* character. Here, for example, is the anti-fascist activist Colin Sparks writing in 1980:

Fascism is a genuinely autonomous tool of the middle classes. Many accounts claim that the radicalism of fascist movements – their attacks upon monopoly finance-capital and 'conspiracies' – are merely camouflage to other ends. This is clearly not the case: the conditions of the mass of fascist supporters mean that they genuinely believe in these slogans and their political activity is designed to implement them.[22]

There is a lot to unpack here, and this we must do if we are to lay bare the inner essence of fascism. It might help to backtrack a little and attempt a definition of class.

A lot of dreadful nonsense is spoken about class. It is not a matter of accent, education, lifestyle, or even, in a narrow sense, occupation and income. Class is an economic process and a social relationship. This is easiest to understand in relation to the two main classes of modern society: the capitalist class and the working class.

Industrialists make a profit by selling the goods produced by the workers they employ. Landlords earn rent on properties leased to workers. Bankers accrue interest on mortgages and other debts owed by workers. In every case, an economic process of exploitation is under way: wealth is being transferred from the working population – whether as workers at the point of production or as customers/debtors at the point of consumption – to those who own property.

Implicit in this is a social relationship: between boss and worker, landlord and tenant, banker and debtor – that is, between exploiter and exploited. This is the essence of class. The facts are simple and undeniable. The rich could not be rich unless the poor worked for them and got screwed: the wealth at the top has to come from somewhere.

What complicates the picture – and creates the basis for endless obfuscation by sociologists, journalists, and politicians – is the existence of intermediate layers between the capitalist class and the working class, and the existence of gradations within each of the latter. This means that, on a superficial view, it looks as if society is made up of many classes – as many as you like, in fact, since it all depends on where you choose to draw the lines.

There is work for cohorts of academics on six-figure research budgets here. One recent example is a BBC survey of 160,000 people which concluded with the 'discovery' that Britain is now divided into *seven* classes – the elite, the established middle-class, new affluent workers, the technical middle-class, emergent service workers, the traditional working-class, and the precariat.[23]

This is unscientific hokum. These distinctions have no theoretical basis: they are pop sociology for dinner parties. It is the vital matter of social class reduced to a parlour game (complete with 'calculator' to enable you to identify your own 'class').

What is true, however, is that the gradations within classes can give rise to contrary social pressures and divergent political affiliations. This is especially true in the middle class, which, by definition, stands between the two main classes.

A useful distinction can be made between what might be called the 'old middle-class' and the 'new middle-class'. The former comprises a multiplicity of small businesspeople, including farmers, local traders, petty contractors, freelance professionals, and the proverbial self-employed plumber, while the latter consists of salaried employees who work in higher level administrative, managerial, and professional roles.

The upper levels of the middle class tend to be personally ambitious and aspirational: their hope is to make money or earn promotion and thereby advance their social position through individual effort. The lower levels, on the other hand, merge into the upper levels of the working class. Professional work in education, medicine, engineering, social welfare, and government administration, for example, involves occupational hierarchies which span the class divisions, with highly paid managers at the top and trade unionists at the base.

The critical point for our analysis of fascism is this: there is no 'middle way' in politics corresponding to a middle-class social position. There are two main classes in society, and all social movements must reflect, in however vague and diffuse a way, the interests of either the capitalist class – 'the system' – or of the working class – whose interests would be served by overthrowing the system and ending exploitation by the rich and the corporations. There cannot be a separate 'middle-class' interest. No reconfiguration of society that might constitute some sort of *Daily Telegraph* reader's nirvana is conceivable.

This means that fascism cannot be defined as a movement of the middle class *per se*, since no distinct set of middle-class interests that it might serve can be said to exist. Fascism might be considered middle-class only in the looser sense that it has particular appeal to middle-class people and tends to attract middle-class members, activists, and voters. But this does not get us very far, since the same could be said of most political parties, certainly nowadays, in that higher levels of political engagement tend to be correlated with higher levels of education.

This brings us to a critical analytical issue. Political parties are never direct expressions of class interest. They do not function in the same way as, say, employers' organisations (on one side) or trade unions (on the other). Parties are alliances that seek to garner broad support by putting forward general programmes. They always do this in the concrete circumstances of a particular conjuncture, in competition with other parties, and in relation to 'the issues of the day'.

Fascism, therefore, is a direct expression of the interests of neither big business nor the middle class. To try and understand it in this way is mechanical and reductionist.

To unravel the complexities of political life, we must have proper regard for the fact that everything is connected with everything else, that all social phenomena are shaped by interaction with opposing forces. The implication is that we cannot separate our analysis of a political party from the wider context in which it operates. More than that: context is a necessary part of any definition. Fascism, then, is not the 'tool' of a social class: it is an artefact of the conjuncture as a whole – that is, of the state of affairs at a particular time, in a particular place; specifically, of the balance of class forces in a context of severe capitalist crisis.

Before proceeding further, a word must be said about the 'lumpenproletariat' referred to in Trotsky's description of fascism above, since a version of this conception arises in contemporary discourse. The term was first used by Marx in descriptions of European political events in the mid 19th century. Here is one of his characterisations of this social group:

Alongside decayed debauchees of doubtful origin and uncertain means of subsistence, alongside ruined and adventurous scions of the bourgeoisie, there were vagabonds, discharged soldiers, discharged criminals, escaped galley-slaves, swindlers, confidence tricksters, homeless idlers, pickpockets, sleight-of-hand experts, gamblers, pimps, brothel-keepers, porters, pen-pushers, organ-grinders, rag-and-bone merchants, knife-grinders, tinkers, and beggars; in short, the whole indeterminate fragmented mass, tossed backwards and forwards, which the French call *la bohème*.[24]

It is perhaps a classic description of the presumed social composition of a reactionary mob in an early industrial city. It does not help us very much. The implication is that a valid socio-logical distinction can be made between a 'respectable' working-class and a 'rough' underclass of the destitute and desperate.

Versions of this caricature have resurfaced in recent aca-demic and political discussion. Here, for example, is a US soci-ologist's definition of the 'underclass' in 1987:

[It comprises] that heterogeneous grouping of families and individuals who are outside the mainstream of the American occupational system. Included...are indi-viduals who lack training and skills and either experi-ence long-term unemployment or are not members of the labour force, individuals who are engaged in street crime and other forms of aberrant behaviour, and fami-lies that experience long-term spells of poverty and/or welfare dependency.[25]

The concept of the underclass fits neatly with the schematic conceptions of class we criticised above. It implies a distinct class group, largely sealed off from the rest of society, vegetat-ing in the lower depths, sustaining itself on the basis of state

benefits, casual jobs, and petty crime: 'scroungers' as opposed
to 'strivers'. Needless to say, this essentially ideological – as
opposed to scientific – construct is routinely racialised. What
politicians like to call 'hardworking families' are encouraged
to believe they are threatened by a brooding mass of (dark-
skinned) foreigners, criminals, and fraudsters.

In reality, no such group exists. Many working-class people
experience periods of unemployment, poverty, and even home-
lessness at certain points in their lives. People in regular full-time
employment live on the same estates as people dependent on benefits. The latter will include carers, single-mothers, the disabled,
and the elderly; and also people forced into low-paid or part-time
jobs because they cannot get anything else. Even people in long-
term unemployment will usually be in families where others are in
work. As one recent survey of poverty in Britain reported:

> Between 2011 and 2014, nearly one-third of the UK pop-
> ulation experienced relative income poverty at least once.
> Groups most vulnerable to poverty are older people,
> people who left school without any formal education,
> women, and people in single-person households.[26]

The concept of an 'underclass' – or 'lumpenproletariat' –
is a trick of the light: apparent in a passing glance, it vanishes
under close scrutiny.

Trotsky came closest to a sociological description of fascism when he occasionally referred to it as 'human dust'.[27] He
never really developed this idea, and he seems to have been
unaware that it was difficult to square with his interpretation
of fascism as a movement of 'the crazed petty-bourgeoisie and
bands of the declassed and demoralised lumpenproletariat'. We
wish to develop it here, for we think it helps a great deal.

Some parties are more closely associated with specific
social classes than others. Though the Tory Party seeks support from the electorate as a whole, it is closely tied to the rich,

big business, and the middle class. In the same way, the Labour Party has always been closely associated with the trade unions and the working class.

These are examples of what Marx meant when he distinguished between 'class for itself' and 'class in itself'. The first describes a situation where a social class becomes organised and conscious in pursuit of its own interests. The latter refers to the mere existence of a class, as a sociological fact, irrespective of whether or not it acts and thinks as such. What we have here is an example of the distinction between 'agency' and 'structure' – between members of a class operating as conscious 'social actors' and people who simply subsist at a particular social level.

But what about a situation in which a deep and protracted crisis tears society apart and makes life intolerable for growing numbers of people? Those organised as a class force may become increasingly energised – they may move sharply to the left, towards more radical solutions to society's problems, perhaps drawing many newly aroused people into action alongside them. But what if the Left fails to give an effective lead and act as a magnet for society's discontents? What then?

The answer is that the discontents may flow to the right. 'If you place a ball on top of a pyramid,' Trotsky explained, 'the slightest impact can cause it to roll down either to the left or the right.' In Germany in 1932, the forces of socialism and fascism were equally poised. In the US presidential election of 2016, Bernie Sanders might have secured the Democratic nomination and gone on to win the presidency. But when Hitler became chancellor, and when Trump was elected president, the ball definitely rolled down to the right.

In both cases – and in every other case where far-right politics have become a mass phenomenon – it is not that people rally to nationalism, racism, and authoritarianism as an expression of their class interest. They rally to it as individuals, as 'human dust'; and it is the movement itself that binds the dust together, gives it cohesion, and turns it into a political force.

This explains the centrality of fascism's leadership cult, its idealisation of the fascist movement and its values, its insistence upon the existence of a 'race', a 'nation', a 'people' that must be united against its enemies. Only by such devices may human dust be swept into a pile. Only thus may the atomised human debris of capitalist crisis be accumulated into a reactionary power to stand against the danger of revolution from below.

Fascism, then, is a somewhat random concentration of people around a rather specific set of ideas. What are those ideas?

## BLOOD AND SOIL: THE IDEOLOGY OF FASCISM

### NATIONALISM

The late Eric Hobsbawm, the great historian of 19th century Europe, saw the origins of the modern world in a 'dual revolution' between 1789 and 1848.[28] The French Revolution transformed world politics, sweeping away an *ancien régime* based on absolute monarchy, feudal landownership, and Catholic dogma, replacing it with a new bourgeois order based on capitalism, nationalism, and citizenship. The Industrial Revolution, pioneered in Britain, unleashed the full potential of capitalism, as machines and the factory system delivered unprecedented increases in output, and a dynamic process of exponential economic growth developed.

The political and industrial revolutions were closely intertwined. The territory of the modern nation-state – where feudal restrictions were abolished in favour of *laissez-faire* entrepreneurship – provided the unified market-place needed by a fast-expanding industrial economy. Nationalism and capitalism were bedfellows.

The state played a key role. It enforced the laws which regulated capitalist competition, provided essential infrastructure like roads, canals, and railways, suppressed strikes and popular protests, and provided the military power to advance capitalist interests abroad.

The last point must be stressed. Globalisation is not new. Capitalism has always sought raw materials, labour-power, markets, and investment opportunities overseas. The great merchant companies of the 16th century were as 'global' in their outlook as City of London bankers today. So to nationalism and capitalism, we may add a third bedfellow: imperialism.

There is a fourth: racism. This requires further discussion, beginning with its roots in nationalism.

The 'nation' is an artificial construct of the historical process. Where borders come to lie – who is included, who excluded – results from accidents of diplomatic intrigue and armed conflict in the past. Germany, for example, was united only in 1871. It was then dismembered in 1919, reassembled between 1936 and 1941, divided in two in 1945, and then reassembled again in 1990.

There is nothing exceptional in this. A series of chronological snapshots of the political geography of Europe since the dual revolution would show the constant flux as countries form, break up, lose territory, gain territory, and are thereby reconfigured into new entities. Between 1991 and 1999, for example, the unified state of Yugoslavia broke up, and a succession of ferocious sectarian wars raged across much of its former territory before five successor states emerged; since which time, two more have formed, so that what was once a single country is now seven.

Nations, in short, are artificial constructs. This means that national identity and sentiment can be kindled only by recourse to myth-making and what Hobsbawm called 'the invention of tradition'.[29]

This brings us to that fourth bedfellow – racism – that nestles alongside capitalism, nationalism, and imperialism. Inherent in any attempt to define a 'nation' or 'people' is the contrast with other 'nations' and 'peoples'. Indeed, as modern philosophers have taught us, our entire perception of social reality is based on perception of difference. The nation-state, with its borders and political control over a defined geographical space, gives rise to 'difference' based on language, custom, history, tradition, and myth. Nationalism then becomes the idea that those who live within the borders of a nation-state (or those who aspire to create such a nation-state) have common interests vis-à-vis those who live elsewhere; and, by extension, that these common interests override any differences that may exist *within* the nation-state. What matters most, from a nationalist perspective, is that we are 'British', or 'German', or 'American', or whatever: not whether we are rich or poor, capitalist or worker, landlord or tenant.

But there is a fatal flaw: while the nation is an artificial construct, class is not. When British and German workers in uniform killed one another in the trenches of the First World War, they served not their own interests, but those of their rulers. National flags, as Indian writer and activist Arundhati Roy put it, 'are bits of coloured cloth that governments use first to shrink-wrap people's minds and then as ceremonial shrouds to bury the dead'.[30]

The danger for the system is always that real *sectional* interests will assert themselves over 'virtual' *national* interests; that people will organise and fight on a class basis, and thereby shatter the pretence of common interest between rich and poor. Nationalism – let us define it here as identification with a nation-state and a constructed 'nation' and 'national identity' – is a façade of icons and symbols, easily dissolved by the visceral experience of class exploitation and struggle. One reason that racism in some form is a key component of fascist ideology is that it gives greater ideological density – and therefore political resilience – to nationalism.

RACISM
The form and degree of racism may vary. German Nazism and Italian Fascism represent two extremes. Anti-semitic racism was so central to Nazi ideology that resources were eventually diverted on a massive scale to industrialised genocide. By contrast, anti-semitism and other forms of overt racism played almost no role in the politics of Italy between 1919 and 1943. The emphasis was on Mussolini the strong leader, a resurgent Italian nation, the modernisation of the economy, the building up of the armed forces, and the creation of a new 'Roman' empire.

But there was an irreducible racist core even here. The colonial conquest of Ethiopia in 1935, for example, was justified in traditionally racist terms. Ethiopia was portrayed as a 'barbarian country', the Italian invasion as the advent of 'civilisation'. Mussolini's speeches at the time were littered with references to Italy's imperial past, her present-day mission, and her future role in the world. The Italians had achieved 'a grade of national maturity'; they had never before revealed 'such force of character'; they were 'worthy of their past'; and, having 'created an empire with their blood', they would 'fertilise it with their work' and 'defend it with their weapons'.[31]

This amounts to a racialisation of both nationalism and imperialism. The first flows from the logic of the latter two. Here is how Martin Webster, one of the leaders of the (fascist) National Front in Britain during the 1970s, put it in a TV interview:

> ...we are a racialist front. You must understand what that means. It means that we support the concept of the nation as the means whereby our society is to be organised, and we believe the only rational basis for having nations is some kind of a degree of ethnic homogeneity.[32]

Racism, more or less explicit, provides nationalism with its real substance. 'Our' national interests must predominate over 'theirs' – so runs the subtext – because we are right, we are moral, we are civilised, we are superior.

As well as substantiating nationalism, racism has other important functions. It conjures into existence an alien 'Other' – whether threatening us at home or challenging us abroad (or, more usually, both) – against whom the national community must unite. The social misery at the base of the system is real enough, but the true explanation of this must remain hidden if the 'nation' is to endure, since class war against the exploiters would sunder national unity. The enemy – the cause of our woes – must, therefore, be some other. Racism supplies that other, and elevates it into an all-pervasive threat. For the Nazis, it was 'an international Jewish conspiracy' that linked Wall Street (capitalism) and Moscow (communism) in an all-out global effort to destroy the 'Aryan' race.

Let us consider another example in more detail. The American Ku Klux Klan can be regarded as one of history's most successful fascisms.[33] In its first incarnation, between 1865 and 1868, it prevented a 'radical reconstruction' of the defeated Confederate states after the American Civil War, driving the newly liberated slaves back into servile subordination to their former masters. It was a mass counter-revolutionary movement of up to half a million members based on white-supremacism and anti-black racism.[34]

Re-founded half a century later – partly in response to the success of D W Griffith's blockbuster cinema epic *The Birth of a Nation*, a deeply racist film that portrayed black men as rapists and white-hooded klansmen as heroes – the 'Second Klan' played a key role in defending the United States against revolution during the wave of radicalisation between 1917 and 1923. The Klan was for America what the Black Hundreds were for Russia, the *Freikorps* for Germany, and the Blackshirts for Italy.[35] This time, anti-black racism was less important: the emphasis was on anti-communist, anti-union, anti-semitic, anti-Catholic, and anti-migrant agitation. The Second Klan advanced a form of white-supremacism based on a conservative, Anglo-Saxon,

Protestant 'native' identity. Its success was phenomenal: its membership peaked at around four million, its largest rally was 200,000 strong, and it counted 40,000 Protestant ministers in its ranks.[36]

The 'Third Klan' peaked in the 1960s, though membership was restricted to the Southern states and never numbered more than about 40,000. Facing a 'second reconstruction' – the attempt of the Civil Rights Movement to end segregation in the South – the Klan switched back to a strong focus on anti-black racism, laced with anti-communism and general antipathy to the progressive movements of the Sixties.[37]

On each occasion, racism was the nucleus of the Ku Klux Klan's white-supremacist nationalism. The 'nation' was synonymous with what would later be called 'WASPs' (white Anglo-Saxon Protestants), and the main enemy was always inside the nation-state, attacking the social order and the body politic from within – so it was the black freed-people of 1865, the Catholic and Yiddish immigrants of 1919, and the black civil-rights protestors of 1960 who constituted the respective racial Others.

In the century between 1865 and 1965, the Ku Klux Klan kindled the flames of race hatred in America and periodically fanned it into the blaze of a racial civil war. At the peak of its power, the Invisible Empire of the Ku Klux Klan was a veritable state within the state, terrorising the oppressed, intimidating activists, overriding the law, moulding public opinion, pulling the political strings.

If racism gives substance to nationalism, it also gives voice to alienation. Capitalism seeks to break society down into its smallest atoms, into individual workers and consumers. It favours a ruthless competition for jobs that serves to keep wages low (and, incidentally, a neurotic obsession with shopping that serves to keep demand high). The capitalist ideal is a war of all against all, a desperate struggle to survive, in which there is no collective resistance, and the balance of power between capital and labour remains permanently tilted in the former's favour.

This war of all against all – in competition for jobs, homes, promotion, more pay, higher living standards, decent medical care, a good education – is the material basis for racism. Its actual form is determined by historical tradition: by the fracture lines that have emerged in the past and that are prone to gape open again in periods of crisis.

We are using 'racism' in a generic sense, not in a biological, or even a cultural sense; so we include any division on the basis of race, nationality, ethnicity, religion, or whatever at the base of society. We do this because the concrete *form* of racism is secondary to its social *function*. We have encountered one example already: the anti-Catholicism of the Ku Klux Klan, which performed exactly the same function in relation to immigrant communities originating from southern Europe as anti-black racism in relation to Afro-Americans in the southern United States.

The dominant form of European racism in the 1930s – anti-semitism – was, in fact, a compound of biological racism (even though no Jewish 'race' actually exists), cultural racism (where East European Yiddish stereotypes predominated), and anti-Judaic religious bigotry. The dominant form of European racism today – Islamophobia – is also a compound. Anti-Islamic religious bigotry is entwined with the explicit notion that Muslims collectively constitute an alien cultural community and the usually implicit assumption that they are dark-skinned.

Attempts to define racism narrowly are pointless exercises in semantics. Fascist activity is not determined by the distinction between colour, culture, and creed. Among the *dramatis personae* of the capitalist crisis is the alien Other of fascist discourse. The oppressed minorities selected to play this role vary from place to place and from time to time. The role is always the same.

The targeted minority becomes the lightning-rod of society's discontents. The despair, frustration, and bitterness at the base of the system is organised and canalised by the fascist movement, and turned into a political force that puts the fascist leadership on the path to power. That journey involves cutting deals with traditional elites, and, if it reaches its destination, the assumption of control over the capitalist state-apparatus. Fascist attacks on the rich, the corporations, and the institutions of the state must, therefore, be muted. The primary ideological mechanism which fascism uses to negotiate the contradiction between its anti-elite rhetoric and its manoeuvring for power within the existing system is attacks on scapegoats.

The most complete expression of this was the 'international Jewish conspiracy' of Nazi mythology. The financiers, the exploiters, the big capitalists wrecking small businesses were 'Jewish'. The communists and the union organisers were also 'Jewish'. Germany's defeat in 1918 and the Versailles peace imposed in 1919 – with its territorial dismemberment, its reparations payments, its military restrictions – these were the work of 'international Jewry'. Wall Street was run by 'Jewish' bankers. Moscow was controlled by 'Jewish' communists. This fevered world-view provided the ideological framework for the anti-semitic activism of Nazi street-thugs in 1932 and, ultimately, for the industrialised genocide of the SS in 1944.

Implicit racism defines the 'nation' and helps justify militarism, imperialism, and war. Explicit racism is a mechanism for managing society's discontents and for dividing the working class against itself. Racism is the ideological workhorse of fascism.

## SEXISM

The alien Other is not the only enemy against which fascism mobilises. The 'nation' is also threatened by the breakdown of the family, the emancipation of women, and the sexuality of LGBT people.

The family is one of the building-blocks of capitalist society. Though it has changed radically over time, especially in the last half century or so, the family remains essential to the low-cost maintenance, reproduction, and socialisation of the labour force. It is central to each of the following social processes: satisfying the basic physical and emotional needs of workers; providing the money, time, and effort involved in rearing children; caring for the elderly and the disabled; and supporting students, the unemployed, and other family dependants.

All of these processes could be collectivised. Some are to a limited extent. But the expense when this is done amounts to a tax on the system and therefore becomes a target for right-wing attacks on 'profligate spending', 'the nanny state', 'welfare dependency', and so on. Better, from a capitalist perspective, that the working-class family should carry the burden than that the state should spend on nurseries, care homes, social services, and adequate grants, benefits, and pensions.

Collective provision would have another deleterious consequence for the system: it would sharply reduce privatised consumption and therefore economic demand. The individual family household is an exceptionally high-cost unit, each requiring a full array of home, car, furnishings, gadgets, clothing, food, heating, light, and so on. The family-centred frenzy to consume is, moreover, sustained by an anxious competitiveness among households fostered by a massive corporate sales-effort. Consumers are encouraged to shop for the products that will make them classy, affluent, fashionable, educated, and sexy; the message is that you are what you have. This all-pervasive social disease of alienated consumption is centred on the household. Capitalism needs the family as a mass market.

The family has other advantages for the system: it is a mechanism of social and ideological control. Its very existence means that society is broken down into the smallest of atoms – family households – and that social life is therefore largely reduced to privatised consumption and personal ambition. It is difficult to exaggerate the significance of this. Every problem – earning a living, finding a home, paying the bills, getting into university, accessing medical care, and so on – becomes a problem of the individual and her family. Despite the fact that all of these problems are *socially* determined – employment opportunities, the affordability of housing, charges for utilities, the cost of education, the availability of health services – they are experienced as *private* matters. Thus the family hard-wires privatised ways of thinking about collective matters into our consciousness.

It is this, as much as anything, that makes the modern family an incubator of conformity and conservatism. Many families are still blighted by traditional patriarchal authority. But even in relatively liberal households – where parental roles are less gender-specific and parental authority less repressive – an irreducible core of top-down control and socialisation endures. Parents have power because they are providers and their children dependants. And they exercise that power in various ways, sometimes to satisfy their own psychological needs, sometimes in what they consider 'the best interests' of their children, which tends to mean encouraging or enforcing behaviour that conforms to the imperatives of the social order. Even the most liberal parents can hardly avoid being the prototype of the teacher, the office supervisor, and the police officer.

These are the reasons that the family is the political property of the Right, whereas personal freedom, not least sexual freedom, is the political property of the Left. They are the reasons that the Far Right is sexist, even misogynist, and homophobic.

The Nazi attitude to women was summed up by the slogan *Kinder, Küche, Kirche* ('children, kitchen, church'). As Hitler explained in a speech to an audience of Nazi women in September 1934:

> If the man's world is said to be the state, his struggle, his readiness to devote his powers to the service of the community, then it may perhaps be said that the woman's is a smaller world. For her world is her husband, her family, her children, and her home...

The Nazis gave traditional gender roles an extra twist: German women – like Spartan women – were considered the breeding-machines of a 'master-race' of men:

> The struggle that the man makes in the struggle of his nation, the woman makes in the preservation of the nation in individual cases. What the man gives in courage on the battlefield, the woman gives in eternal self-sacrifice, in eternal pain and suffering. Each child that a woman brings into the world is a battle, a battle waged for the existence of her people.[38]

Challenges to the family and the patriarchal order can sometimes provoke paroxysms of rage against 'loose women' and 'degenerate homosexuals'. Fascist thugs often target women activists and LGBT people. Fascist regimes often use the state apparatus to hedge women's lives around with restrictions on employment, legal rights, and access to contraception, abortion, and nurseries. The Nazis put 100,000 gay men into concentration-camps, many of whom were later exterminated among the 12 million victims of the Holocaust.

## AUTHORITARIANISM

One key component of fascist ideology remains for consideration. In its rise to power, fascist propaganda is anti-elite, anti-Establishment, anti-system. Society is in crisis, people's lives are falling apart, and the existing political set-up seems paralysed, indifferent, complacent, probably corrupt, certainly incapable of providing solutions; in short, not fit for purpose. The fascist demagogue offers a Cleansing of the Augean Stables, a sweeping away of the old, failed, self-serving liberal elite, and its replacement with a regime formed of a new, younger, stronger generation.[39]

The would-be dictator likes to present himself as somehow above politics, parties, and the pettiness of the parliamentary game – as the embodiment of some sort of non-partisan 'national' programme of redemption and regeneration. This pose is, of course, a fake, for the 'cleansing' is bound to be superficial: the fascists want control of the existing state-apparatus and the cooperation of big business in order to implement policies of national unity, economic regeneration, rearmament, and war.

But in one crucial respect, the anti-system rhetoric is for real: the fascists aim to curtail liberal parliamentary democracy and associated personal freedoms.

The capitalist system knows many forms of political rule, of which liberal parliamentary democracy is perhaps the ideal, since it tends to maximise consent and stability by offering a semblance of popular power. Better that the rule of capital and the state be veiled by elections, a free press, and public debate than that it take the naked form of the dominance of police and money. But, as Trotsky put it, 'the wires of democracy cannot take too high a social voltage'.[40] If the circuits are blown – if the economic collapse deepens, if social distress increases, if political tensions produce paralysis – then the age of the 'strong man' dawns. The system in crisis seeks another way to rule.

For fascism, authoritarianism is natural and inevitable. It is in revolt against the Enlightenment and the revolutionary ideals of liberty, equality, and freedom.[41] It rejects civil, democratic, and human rights, for they enshrine the freedom of the individual, of oppressed minorities, and of sectional interests. It opposes the liberal state, with its balance of powers, its legal protections, its ready tolerance of difference and disagreement, for these, in effect, institutionalise social divisions. Not least, the liberal state accords rights, a voice, a place in society to the alien Other, the canker in the body politic of the 'nation'.

If the crisis renders social tensions unmanageable within a liberal democratic framework, the fascist elevation of an *imagined* 'race', or 'nation', or 'people' into the central principle of political organisation necessitates the suppression of *real* sectional interests – above all, the interests of the working class, as embodied in labour organisation and socialist politics. Fascism cannot permit free play to the struggle of classes and parties, of minorities and campaigns, for to do so is to deny the unity of the 'nation'. Lacking any real existence in social life, the unity of the 'nation' can be imposed only by diktat from above.

Liberal democracy manages the tension between nation and class in periods when compromise is possible. Fascism is the triumph of nation over class: it is the authoritarian imposition of a fake 'national unity' in a period of acute social tension. Leader cult and dictatorship are therefore inherent in fascist politics. They are the essential mechanism for overriding the class struggle.

## PSYCHOTIC RAGE:
## THE MASS PSYCHOLOGY OF FASCISM

'Imagine a furious horde,' wrote an appalled Vietnamese immigrant describing a Ku Klux Klan lynching in 1924.

> Fists clenched, eyes bloodshot, mouths foaming, yells, insults, curses... This horde is transported with the wild delight of a crime to be committed without risk...
>
> Imagine in this human sea a flotsam of black flesh pushed about, beaten, trampled underfoot, torn, slashed, insulted, tossed hither and thither, bloodstained...
>
> In a wave of hatred and bestiality, the lynchers drag the black to a woods or public place. They tie him to a tree, pour kerosene over him, cover him with flammable material. While waiting for the fire to be kindled, they smash his teeth, one by one...
>
> The black is cooked, browned, burned. But he deserves to die twice instead of once. He is therefore hanged, or more exactly, what is left of his corpse is hanged...

When everybody has had enough, the corpse is brought down. The rope is cut into small pieces which will be sold for three or five dollars each. Souvenirs and lucky charms quarrelled over by the ladies...

While on the ground, stinking of fat and smoke, a black head, mutilated, roasted, deformed, grins horribly and seems to ask the setting sun, 'Is this civilisation?'[42]

Not only is it not civilisation; it is not any kind of normality. It is a collective madness, a mass psychotic rage, a grotesque 'return of the repressed'.[43] Similar examples from the history of fascism would fill a library. Again and again, fascism displays its ability to unleash some monster from the depths of the human unconscious. How are we to explain this?

A number of attempts have been made to marry Marxist theory and Freudian psychoanalysis, with varying degrees of success. These endeavours have rarely attracted much attention on the Left – except perhaps for a time in the 1960s – even in relation to a phenomenon like fascism, that seems to cry out for such an approach. For who can doubt that fascism is not only a disease of the body politic and social order, but also of the human mind? Its deeply irrational character, its open defiance of scientific thought, its neurotic obsession with myths, icons, and 'blood and soil' mysticism, the primeval brutality of its many atrocities, all this makes it an obvious case of mass psychopathology.

Seminal work on the psychology of fascism was done by the Marxist-Freudian psychoanalyst Wilhelm Reich in the 1930s.[44] Reich summed up his view in these words: 'Fascist mentality is the mentality of the 'little man' who is enslaved and craves authority and is at the same time rebellious.'[45]

Reich regarded the patriarchal-authoritarian family as both the crucible of this contradictory mind-set and the model for the authoritarian-fascist state. He considered an oppressive sexual morality – enforced mainly by the structures and strictures of the family – to be a feature of all class societies, partly due to preoccupation with private property, rights of inheritance, and therefore control over the sexuality of women, and partly because psychic repression facilitated social control by making people neurotic, insecure, and thus malleable and submissive.

The basic mechanism at work here had been discovered by Sigmund Freud a generation before. The repression of sexual desire (libido) gives rise to various neurotic complexes – lust/guilt in relation to sex, fear/craving in relation to authority, rebellion/conformity in social interactions, and so on. Reich's explicit 'politicisation' of this paradigm was a major theoretical advance – though it is now clear that the primacy he gave to the patriarchal-authoritarian family, which he called 'political reaction's germ-cell', was overstated.[46] The more 'liberal-egalitarian' family (if one can call it that) of the last half century does not appear to have reduced society's capacity for 'political reaction' to the degree Reich might have anticipated. So let us attempt to update the mass psychology of fascism a little.

To do this, we need to broaden our conceptual framework – from the minutiae of family structures and gender roles to the whole nexus of social-control mechanisms within which the family is embedded in class society. Erich Fromm's work is of assistance here. He argued that 'fear of freedom' is a generic human condition – at least in class societies with repressive social structures and sexual mores – such that the experience of freedom is liable to intensify feelings of anxiety and a concomitant craving for authority, order, certainty, and the sense of security and safety these afford.[47]

The deepest psychic root of this 'fear of freedom' is the birth trauma – the single most searing experience of human existence: the abrupt, violent ejection of the infant from the warmth and security of the womb. The separation anxiety imprinted on the psyche at this moment remains throughout life. It provides the blueprint for sexual desire, family intimacy, human sociability in general, the craving to 'belong', the desolation of loneliness. Whereas Reich's conception is of a rather specific guilt/authority neurosis, Fromm's is of a more generic separation/security neurosis.

Both insights are useful, and both can inform an understanding of the mass psychology of fascism. It can be thought of as an infantile flight from the anxiety generated by increased personal freedom, independence, creativity, and self-expression, towards some sort of substitute womb, or mother, or childhood family, as represented by a traditionally structured, morally repressive, authoritarian social order.

By this mechanism, a particular type of split personality is socially constructed. On the one hand, the individual develops what Reich calls 'character armour', a set of traits which have a repressive function and give rise to 'biologic rigidity, incapacity for freedom, a mechanical-authoritarian view of life'.[48] This, he argues, drawing on Freud's phasing of childhood sexual development, involves regression from the 'genital' phase to an earlier 'narcissistic' or 'anal' phase.

Genital sexuality, in which the libido is projected towards others, seeking satisfaction in union with them, is object-focused and therefore the psychic basis of love, friendship, sociability, team-building, solidarity, compassion, and all other forms of cooperative human interaction. Both narcissism and anality, on the other hand, are associated with a wide range of subject-focused disorders, from the excessive egotism and selfishness of the narcissistic personality to the obsessive compulsions of the anally fixated. Fear of responsibility and fear of freedom – and therefore the repressive-authoritarian personality – have their roots here.[49]

Repression, rigidity, character armour: here is one of the two foundation-blocks of the fascist individual. Mysticism, Reich maintains, is the other. In his most blunt formulation, he writes that 'mysticism is nothing other than unconscious longing for orgasm'.[50] His point is that the character armour of the repressive-authoritarian personality is a defence against unconscious drives and wishes that continue to operate, seeking some form of expression and sublimated satisfaction. This is evident in fascism's mystical elevation of symbols, rituals, rallies, leader-worship, and military glory, and in its spinning of fantasies from the concepts of race, nation, and folk-community. 'The Prussian military parades,' Reich explains,

> betray all the characteristics of a mystical and mechanical man. Human mysticism, which thus represents the last traces of vitality, also became the fountainhead of mechanical sadism in Hitlerism. From the deepest sources of biologic functioning still remaining, the cry for 'freedom' wins through again and again, notwithstanding all the rigidity and enslavement... The various cries for freedom are as old as the ossification of the human plasma.[51]

Not only does this provide us with an understanding at the level of individual psychology of the appeal of 'strong leaders', restrictions on civil liberties, and repressive action against dissidents; it also leads us to an understanding of the mass psychotic rage which sometimes erupts inside a fascist movement.

Neurosis arises when social reality triggers feelings of doubt, anxiety, and inner conflict that prevent the individual from acting decisively and effectively. Psychosis arises when social reality becomes wholly unmanageable and is displaced by an alternative 'virtual' reality, such that the individual may well act with decision and effect, but in ways that are dysfunctional and may be destructive. In this case, anxiety can turn into irrational rage and violence. Frequently, the basic complex – the flight from freedom to authoritarianism – is conflated with one or more secondary complexes to create a powerful cocktail of misdirected mental energy (known technically, in psychoanalysis, as 'cathexis').

In the minds of the socially marginal, the personally inadequate, the sexually insecure – people who sense that in some way they are 'losers' – frustration and resentment can accumulate. When attacks upon external targets are legitimised – on migrants, women, Jews, gays, Catholics, communists, Roma, Muslims – targets that may symbolise hidden fears of failure, rejection, emasculation – targets that may trigger deep-rooted anxiety complexes – the result can be an explosion of psychotic rage. Such rage, when canalised and politicised, often takes a collective form, passing like an electric current back and forth through the crowd, gathering force as it does so. This is 'the return of the repressed' with a vengeance – libidinal energy converted into murderous violence.

## SUMMARY

We set out at the beginning of this chapter to define fascism. We are now in a position to do this.

Since 'the dual revolution' of 1789-1848 – the political and industrial revolutions which created the modern world – two great clusters of ideas, corresponding to society's two great classes, the capitalist class and the working class, have stood opposed to one another. The most extreme expressions of these opposing clusters are fascism and revolutionary socialism.

The right-wing nexus is composed of an irrational hotchpotch – a bundle of fables, prejudices, and icons. It represents regression to a pre-Enlightenment, pre-scientific way of thinking. It is, in a literal sense, reactionary as opposed to progressive. It is the myths of the 10$^{th}$ century welded to the technology of the 20$^{th}$.

And because it is not rooted in class-conscious human collectives – acting for themselves in the light of reason, deciding for themselves through democratic debate – it taps the ideological sewers at the base of capitalist society, and summons the repressed from the psychic sewers of the human unconscious.

This raw material, in the context of capitalist crisis, it fashions into a counter-revolutionary mass movement to protect the system from the explosive potential inherent in society's accumulating discontents.

Fascism can be understood as the active mobilisation of atomised 'human dust' around the right-wing nexus of nationalism, racism, sexism, and authoritarianism – just as socialism can be considered the active mobilisation of an organised class around the left-wing nexus of internationalism, equality, and democracy.

Formed of human dust, spewing the shit of ages, bloated with psychotic rage, fascism is the mechanism by which a deeply dysfunctional, crisis-ridden system of exploitation and oppression seeks to smash democracy, civil liberties, and any effective resistance to the rule of the rich and the corporations.

# CHAPTER 3
# Fascism in action

Our argument in the previous chapter carries the clear implication that fascism represents a sharp break with 'normal' politics. It is a politics of crisis, of extremes, of unreason, of pathological violence. This is reflected not only in the social composition, ideology, and aims of the fascist movement, but also in its methods. It is to these that we turn in this chapter.

Superficially, much fascist activity seems no different from that of other political movements. Fascists engage in election campaigns and deploy the usual paraphernalia of electioneering – meetings, speeches, media interviews, propaganda stunts, displaying posters, handing out fliers, chalking or painting slogans, door-to-door canvassing, and nowadays, of course, a blitz of texts, emails, tweets, and Facebook posts. Delve deeper, however, and things are not as they seem. For fascists, the aim is not merely to win an election, but to build a movement.

Voting in a liberal parliamentary democracy is the most minimal form of political activity. It takes a citizen less than ten minutes to go into a polling station and cast a ballot, and that, so far as national policy is concerned, is likely to be the full ration of democracy for half a decade. For the rest of the time, government is in the hands of professional politicians and state officials. Unless citizens engage in some form of campaigning – which is actively discouraged, especially when it is effective, which usually involves some form of direct action – voters are, to all intents and purposes, politically inert between elections.

This, of course, suits the system: the power of capital and the state is somewhat camouflaged by this wafer-thin semblance of democratic control, but is not seriously threatened or constrained by it.

Fascism, on the other hand, seeks to arouse and mobilise the human detritus of the capitalist crisis and organise it into an *active* reactionary force. The fascists want to crush the labour movement, the minorities, and the Left, and to dissolve the civil liberties and democratic freedoms enshrined in the liberal parliamentary regime. Fascism is a work of deliberate destruction, for which higher levels of engagement and activity are necessary.

Let us illustrate this by reference to two prominent characteristics of fascist movements in the past: the emphasis on mass rallies; and the creation of paramilitaries and the use of terror against political enemies.

## LITTLE WORMS INTO GREAT DRAGONS

Fascist propaganda makes no appeal to reason or science: it is a cocktail of blood-and-soil mysticism, popular racism, and misdirected rage which seeks to stir emotions. Individuals are not required to think, but to subsume their identity in a great movement of 'national' cleansing and renewal. It is for this reason that the mass rally is so important: it makes the unity, strength, and drive for power of the 'national' movement a living reality for the fascist masses, especially for the party cadre.

Hitler, writing in *Mein Kampf* in 1925, put it starkly: 'mass demonstrations must burn into the little man's soul the conviction that, though a little worm, he is part of a great dragon'.[1] Thus does 'the little man' become powerful. As Richmond Flowers, the Attorney-General of Alabama in the mid 1960s, put it in relation to the Ku Klux Klan: 'When a pitiable misfit puts on his $15 sheet, society can no longer ignore him.'[2]

John Tyndall, the leader of Britain's National Front in the 1970s, developed this idea at some length:

What is it that touches off a chord in the instincts of the people to whom we seek to appeal? It can often be the most simple and primitive thing. Rather than a speech or printed article, it may just be a flag; it may be a marching column; it may be the sound of a drum; it may be a banner; or it may just be the impression of a crowd. None of these things contain in themselves one single argument, one single piece of logic... They are...among the things that appeal to the hidden forces of the human soul.[3]

For Tyndall, this was a recurring theme, reflected in the Front's determination to mount a series of provocative marches, especially through urban areas that were home to large numbers of ethnic-minority people. It was an assertion of power designed to rally, bind together, and activate the human dust of an embryonic fascist movement.

Nothing, absolutely nothing, can be accomplished if the political temperature remains at that level at which the nation has been lulled to sleep while its enemies within and without have plundered its wealth and destroyed its freedom. We have to raise the temperature several degrees if people are to awake and something is to be done.

Enthusiasm has to be created, and that can only be achieved by an appeal of dynamic force which arouses the feelings of the masses just as electric shock-waves arouse life, feeling, and movement in an inert body...

I believe our great marches, with drums and flags and banners, have a hypnotic effect on the public and an immense effect in solidifying the allegiance of our followers, so that their enthusiasm can be sustained.[4]

The famous Nuremberg Rallies, which took place every year between 1933 and 1938, are perhaps the supreme examples of fascist mass demonstrations, with hundreds of thousands of Nazi Party members parading in serried ranks before swastika banners to watch neo-pagan rituals and hear Hitler speak. But far smaller interwar fascisms followed the same model.

When Oswald Mosley launched the British Union of Fascists in 1933, he adopted the *fasces* symbol (later changed to a thunderbolt in a circle), a blackshirt uniform, and a consciously military style of internal organisation. With Lord Rothermere's support – both financial and in press publicity – he then organised three giant rallies at the Albert Hall, Olympia, and White City in 1934.[5] Mosley's biographer describes the scene:

> There were all kinds of spectacle associated with a Mosley rally, especially in the early days: drums, orchestra, communal singing, flags, spotlights, and, of course, the propaganda march to arouse interest. The speaker himself used every kind of oratorical trick to get his message across the footlights – changes in pitch and speed, carefully calculated movements, finger jabbing straight ahead, arms flung apart, crouching low in attack.[6]

The American Ku Klux Klan was much the same. Massed rallies in hooded robes – the largest of them, in Kokomo, Indiana in 1923, was 200,000 strong – centred on speeches and cross-burnings. The effect, again, was to weld 'little worms' into a 'great dragon'. Here is Wyn Craig Wade, the historian of the Klan, describing the mechanism:

> Bathed in warmth, left arms outstretched toward the blazing icon, and voices raised in 'The Old Rugged Cross', Klansmen felt as one body. These were moments they would always remember. To outside foes who witnessed them, cross-burnings were something they would never forget. They were grotesque rituals to be

enacted on American soil. They were spectacles no-one had seen before. And their likes would not be seen again until Berlin of the 1930s.[7]

## 'BLACKSHIRT MAN'

'If we wish to create a power factor,' wrote Hitler in 1925, 'we need unity, authority, and drill. Our purpose must be not to create an army of politicians, but an army of soldiers of the new philosophy'.[8]

Other fascist leaders thought so too. Military organisation was not just a method: it was the realisation of a social ideal – that of a united people marching purposefully towards fulfilment of their historic destiny. The paramilitary organisation of party cadre that was such a feature of interwar fascism was the planned authoritarian state in miniature. The difference between the old parties and the fascists was, according to Mosley,

> not a difference of method or points of policy, but a difference of spirit. And this difference of spirit expresses itself in a different type of man – Blackshirt Man. Fascism excluded the possibility of collaboration with any old party because the psychologies of the old parties are irreconcilable with revolutionary fascism. Fascism can only take members of the old parties and mould them into Blackshirts through the furnace of the struggle for power. The making of Blackshirts and the making of the fascist movement is the preparation in embryo of new Britons and of the new Britain.[9]

Like all political movements, fascism makes distinctions between its core activists, its more passive members, its supporters in the wider population, and the mass of people yet to be won over. But the distinctions, especially between active and passive members, are sharper. In classical fascism, the former tended to be enrolled in uniformed paramilitary groups, and these were often deployed at meetings and on the streets, both to protect fascist events and to attack political rivals.

The prototype was provided by the right-wing militias of ex-servicemen which emerged immediately after the First World War – like the followers of the Italian nationalist adventurer Gabriele D'Annunzio, who seized control of Fiume (in today's Croatia), and the *Freikorps*, formed by German officers as a bulwark against socialist revolution. Post-war Europe was awash with demobilised soldiers habituated to violence. Though many faded back into civilian life, others remained unsettled – rootless, restless, at large – and these often provided early fascism's core cadre.

The model was provided by the pioneer: the National Fascist Party of Benito Mussolini. Tens of thousands of black-shirted *squadristi* ('squad members') were recruited between 1919 and 1922, mainly in the Po Valley of northern Italy, where an alliance of industrial magnates, traditional landowners, and anti-socialist war veterans formed in opposition to a revolutionary working-class movement centred on Italy's 'industrial triangle' of Genoa, Milan, and Turin.

A wave of fascist violence broke the back of both the workers' movement in the cities and a peasant land-reform movement in the countryside. In the first half of 1921, dozens of activists were killed and hundreds of offices, print-works, and meeting places of the unions, the peasant leagues, and the socialist parties were smashed. By the following year, the fascist movement was surging. Some 60,000 unemployed agricultural labourers occupied Ferrara under fascist leadership for two days in May, while 20,000 uniformed *squadristi* took over Bologna for five days in November. When Mussolini launched his 'March on Rome' coup in October 1922, it was led by 35,000 Blackshirts, the vanguard of a party that now claimed 700,000 members.[10]

Fascist paramilitary mobilisation was raised to a higher level in Germany and Spain during the 1930s, partly because of

the depth of the economic crisis after 1929, partly because of
the strength of organised labour. The Nazi SA (*Sturmabteilung*),
the Brownshirts, swelled to 400,000 in the crisis of 1932, when
they were often involved in pitched battles with the 'Red Front
Fighters', the armed militia of the German Communist Party,
and then to a peak of three million following Hitler's assumption of power, as the unions and the left parties were physically
destroyed.[11]

Yet more extreme in its way was the situation in Spain in
1936, where a fascist-backed military coup was met by working-class revolution. What followed was a three-year civil war
of exceptional brutality, in which 200,000 were killed in the
fighting, between 200,000 and 400,000 were massacred, and
another 450,000 forced to flee.[12] Falangist (Spanish fascist)
membership exploded from 75,000 in July 1936 to almost a
million by the end of the year, with 80,000 in arms.[13]

All interwar fascist movements seem to have attempted to
create their own paramilitary wings. Oswald Mosley's 12,000-
strong Olympia rally on 7 June 1934 was attended by some
2,000 Blackshirts, more than half of whom had marched across
London in five columns from the party's headquarters. The
Blackshirts were unleashed on an estimated 500 communist
hecklers who had got into the meeting. Many protestors were
punched, kicked, thrown down steps, and attacked with knuck-
ledusters, cut-throat razors, and wooden clubs.[14]

Fascist violence is multi-purpose. It is used to protect fascist events and disrupt those of political rivals. It offers action
and excitement to the angry, alienated, sometimes mentally disturbed young men the fascists are eager to recruit. It hardens
and consolidates the activist core of the movement. It intimi-
dates fascism's enemies and discourages resistance. It projects
an impression of strength and will. Consider, for example, this
summary of the effects of the Ku Klux Klan's campaign of terror
in the Southern states after the American Civil War:

By 1871, the Klan had rendered Southern Republicans [members of what was at the time a radical abolitionist party], law officers, and military commanders equally helpless. In Texas, General John Reynolds reported that murders of blacks were 'so common as to render it impossible to keep an accurate record of them'. In Mississippi, the Klan was driving nearly every teacher of a black school out of the state. In Georgia and South Carolina, unsolved murders were being committed at the rate of nearly two a month. All over the South, hundreds of blacks were sleeping in the woods for fear of Klan visits to their cabins...[15]

The effects would be felt for a century. The 'Jim Crow' laws – in operation until the mid 1960s – disenfranchised black voters, segregated public spaces and services on racial lines, and impoverished the black population of the Southern states by restricting them to low-paid menial labour and sharecropping tenancies that were little better than slavery.

Emotion and spectacle. Violence and terror. In these respects, fascism represents a break from the political mainstream. This insight helps us get a handle on fascism's highly contradictory character. And it is to this that we now turn – to the tensions inherent in fascism in action.

## SUITS OR BOOTS?

A perennial problem for fascists is that the aims of the fascist leadership and the extremism and violence of the fascist cadre tend to alienate the wider public. This is not simply the general problem that most people most of the time have fairly middle-of-the-road politics. It is more complex.

Even in periods of deep crisis and mass radicalisation, the fascist leadership must continue to hide its politics, since its intention is to cut deals with traditional elites and big business that will make a mockery of its claim to be heading a popular revolt.

Equally problematic is the behaviour of its own hard-core supporters. Active fascists tend to be more racist, violent, and mentally disturbed than passive supporters. On the one hand, these activists are essential party-workers, without whom no real advance is possible; on the other, their behaviour is liable to expose the repellent politics at the heart of the fascist movement and deter mainstream support.

This is the 'suits or boots' dilemma facing all fascist movements. And the closer they come to power, the more acute it becomes, since they must project a sufficiently moderate, respectable image to pull in middle-ground support, while maintaining the enthusiasm of the racist thugs who constitute much of the party cadre. (It is worth commenting here – though we will deal with this in greater detail in the final chapter – that this tension can be exploited by opponents. A key component of anti-fascist strategy has to be to rupture the polite façade and expose the fascist essence.)

Take this example. As Ku Klux Klan membership surged to 100,000 members in the summer of 1921, Klan leaders, hoping for a breakthrough into mainstream national politics, began distancing themselves from the racism and violence of their core supporters. As Grand Wizard William Joseph Simmons explained in testimony before the US Congressional Committee on Rules in 1921:

> I was born among, reared among, and associated with Negroes all my life. I have played with them in the yard of the old home. I have gone fishing with them in the old mountain streams. I have hunted with them... Every Sunday morning I had my class of Negro children and many old Negro men; I taught them their ABCs and how to write... I have always been the friend of the Negro...
>
> And I want to say to my persecutors and the persecutors of this organisation, in all honesty and sincer-

ity...that you do not know what you are doing. You are ignorant of our principles as were those who were ignorant of the character and work of Christ. I cannot better express myself than by saying to you who are persecutors of the Klan and myself, 'Father, forgive you, for you know not what you do.'[16]

This 'popular turn' led to a further surge in Klan support, helped by a powerful alliance with the Fundamentalist Christian Right (with up to 40,000 Protestant pastors becoming Klan members). Even President Harding was sworn in as a member – in what must have been one of the most bizarre ceremonies ever performed in the White House. Membership climbed to one million in late 1921, and reached four million in 1924.[17]

As the organisation grew, its leaders scented power, and that led to tensions at the top. Simmons was ousted and replaced as Grand Wizard by Hiram Wesley Evans. The new regime, not content with denials, tried to curb excesses and clean up the rhetoric. As one local memo recommended:

– DON'T RANT...
– DON'T LIE OR EXAGGERATE...
– DON'T ABUSE THE 'ENEMY'. Nothing is to be gained by raving hysterically about Catholics, Jews, Negroes, Bootleggers, Foreigners, and the like. A scientific, sympathetic, sportsmanlike presentation of facts will win more people and leave you under the necessity of making no apologies to anybody...[18]

Something similar happened to the 'Third Klan' after its defeat by the Civil Rights Movement in the 1960s. The Klan's association with hard racist violence – and the signal failure of its strategy – saw membership plummet from 40,000 in 1965 to 7,000 in 1970. So up-and-coming young Klan leader David Duke set about steering the organisation towards a more moderate, media-savvy, 'political' approach. He smooched his way through the TV studios preaching the new gospel:

> An Imperial Wizard of the KKK with a college degree was an oddity in itself, but a 24-year-old Wizard with a high IQ and the good looks of a soap-opera star was downright confusing. New York talk-show host Stanley Siegel said, 'He sat on my programme and he said the most outrageous things you ever heard about blacks and Jews. The entire time he had this beguiling smile on his face. It was disconcerting.'[19]

It could not last. The shrunken Klan was too dependent on its small remaining cadre of deranged racists – reinforced during the 1970s by embittered Vietnam veterans. By the early 1980s, the Klan was growing again, but on the crest of a new wave of racial violence.

Fascism moves through history with this Jekyll and Hyde split-identity. Sometimes it puts on a suit to go door-to-door and garner votes. Other times it dons a white hood to murder a black man in the night. Two sides of one beast.

## FASCISTS AND CONSERVATIVES

A second problem for any fascist movement is its relationship with traditional elites, the existing state, and big business. Mainstream conservative parties are the natural expression of these interests in liberal parliamentary democracies.

As the crisis intensifies and the fascist movement grows – and especially if the labour movement and the socialist parties are perceived to be a real threat – sections of this core right-wing constituency may defect. But this is never the critical issue: what matters is the establishment of a practical alliance.

So much is this the case that, with one possible exception discussed below, there is, in fact, no such thing as a 'pure' fascist state: to all intents and purposes, all concrete historical examples have been hybrids.

We must stress this point, for it provides the historical underpinning for our concept of 'creeping fascism'. Let us pursue it a little further, then, with a close look at what happened in Italy and Germany.

Italian Prime Minister Giolitti included the Fascists in his 'National Bloc' for the elections of May 1921.[20] Giolitti lost a vote of confidence in February 1922, and his successor, Prime Minister Facta, lost his majority in July the same year, reducing the Italian government to a caretaker administration. Mussolini's 'March on Rome' in October was an attempt to seize power by *coup de main* in the context of this political crisis.

The Left called a general strike in defence of constitutional legality, but it flopped. Facta nonetheless reinforced the Rome garrison and deployed police and railway officials to stop fascist trains reaching the capital. This might have proved decisive. But the political elite was split and a deal was in the offing. Robert Paxton, a leading academic authority on fascism, takes up the story:

> Four hundred police stopped trains carrying 20,000 Blackshirts at three checkpoints... About 9,000 Blackshirts who evaded the checkpoints or continued on foot formed a motley crowd at the gates of Rome on the morning of 28 October, poorly armed, wearing makeshift uniforms, short of food and water, and milling about in a discouraging rain...
>
> At the last moment, King Victor Emmanuel III balked. He decided not to sign Prime Minister Facta's martial-law decree. He refused to call Mussolini's bluff and use the readily available force to exclude the Blackshirts from Rome. He rejected Salandra's last-minute efforts to form a new conservative government without Mussolini, who had by now refused Salandra's offer of a coalition. Instead he offered the prime ministry directly to the young upstart Fascist leader.[21]

What followed was not a sudden lurch into fully fledged dictatorship. In fact, the Italian government remained throughout a 'dual regime' of King and *Duce*, in which Mussolini was constrained by the power of established elites, and his Fascist movement was subordinate to the existing state. Mussolini, in any case, had no desire to be pushed around by regional party bosses; as soon as he had consolidated his rule, he announced that 'the revolution is over', and that state prefects, not fascist party secretaries, were 'the highest authority of the state'. Symbolic, perhaps, of the hybrid nature of the regime throughout its existence is the fact that at the end, just as the King had elevated Mussolini to power in October 1922, it was the King who deposed him in July 1943.[22]

This does not mean that Mussolini did not construct a totalitarian regime: it does mean that it was done in collaboration with traditional elites and by means of the existing state-apparatus. And it was a process. Even as the police and fascist squads were smashing up working-class organisations, the trappings of liberal democracy remained, with socialist and communist deputies free to voice their opinions in the Italian Parliament; and when Giacomo Matteotti, an outspoken socialist deputy, was murdered by fascist thugs in June 1924, the national clamour momentarily destabilised the regime.

Only in November 1926 did Mussolini feel strong enough to complete the destruction of liberal parliamentary democracy. But even now, he acted as the leader of an alliance. Emergency laws were rushed through Parliament, 124 opposition deputies were expelled, and many communists (including Antonio Gramsci) were arrested and imprisoned. Yet this – the formal creation of a totalitarian state – was opposed by only 12 deputies in the lower house. Fascist Italy remained a hybrid state based on a social alliance between the rich, the politicians, and the *squadristi*.[23]

The German case is, in almost all respects, the most extreme. But not even here – except perhaps in the last year of the Third Reich's existence – do we see absolute fascist control. Hitler had attempted to batter his way to power in the 'Beer Hall Putsch' in Munich in November 1923. The police had opened fire and dispersed the Nazis. Hitler had been arrested and imprisoned. The key lesson he learnt was that fascists could not take power by armed insurrection.

The Nazis thereafter adopted a three-pronged strategy: a mass movement of street-fighters to batter the working-class movement; a drive to win mass electoral support within the constitutional mainstream; and secret alliances with landowners, industrialists, and sections of the political establishment. This culminated in President Hindenburg's hoisting of Hitler into power in January 1933, as Germany's traditional elites, shaken by a profound economic, social, and political crisis, rallied to the strongman of the Far Right.

A pattern was established. Nazi Germany was henceforward ruled by what Franz Neumann, the German-Jewish theorist of fascism, called a 'cartel' formed of party, industry, army, and bureaucracy, held together by 'profit, power, prestige, and especially fear'.

The 'normative state' – that is, the rule-bound apparatus of legally constituted authorities, courts, and government departments – continued to operate alongside a new 'prerogative state' represented by parallel party structures like the gauleiters (regional bosses), the SA, and the SS. The relationship between the two was often ill-defined, fluid, and tense; but it was an enduring feature of Nazi rule, almost to the end, even though the party became increasingly dominant as time went on.[24]

'Fascist regimes,' argues Paxton,

> functioned like an epoxy: an amalgam of two very different agents, fascist dynamism and conservative order, bonded by shared enmity toward liberalism and the Left, and a shared willingness to stop at nothing to destroy their common enemies.[25]

This 'amalgam' created the totalitarian regime. An arson attack on the Reichstag on 27 February 1933 was used by the Nazis to proclaim a 'communist plot' and justify emergency laws. President Hindenburg immediately signed these off, suspending all civil liberties, allowing the Nazis to round up 10,000 Communist Party members and inter them in concentration camps. The Nazis then won a rigged general election on 5 March, in which they and their conservative allies, the German National People's Party, won 52% of the popular vote. Hitler then presented an Enabling Act to the new Reichstag – effectively giving him dictatorial powers – and this gained the required two-thirds majority on 23 March, with all conservative and liberal deputies voting in favour.[26]

Events had moved much faster in Germany than in Italy; but this had been a fast-fowarding of the same process – the creation of a totalitarian dictatorship *in collaboration with traditional elites and by means of the existing state-apparatus.*

The alliance remained firm for a decade. It underpinned: the building of an 'autarchic' national economy based on state intervention, infrastructure projects, and rearmament during the mid to late 1930s; an aggressive foreign policy which saw the remilitarisation of the Rhineland in 1936, the annexation of Austria in 1938, the occupation of Czechoslovakia in March 1939, and the invasion of Poland in September 1939; and the Nazi conquest of much of Europe between 1939 and 1942, creating a huge continental empire whose raw materials, factories, labour power, and markets were appropriated by German capital.

Only when the tide of war turned decisively against the Germans at the Battle of Stalingrad in the winter of 1942/43 did the alliance between conservatives and fascists begin to falter. As defeat became increasingly certain, the traditional elite sought a way out by dumping the regime and negotiating a compromise peace. But they found it was too late.

Nazi rule had been strengthened by wartime imperatives, and, in the vast expanses of the occupied East, had crystallised into industrial-scale genocide. The failure of the 'Bomb Plot' of 20 July 1944 – when Hitler narrowly escaped assassination at the hands of a conspiracy of high-ranking officers – merely strengthened the grip of the SS and goaded the regime into a final, deranged, apocalyptic reign of terror.

Ian Kershaw has identified a qualitative shift in the final year of the Third Reich, one that, in our view, represents the most absolute expression of fascism, in which the alliance with traditional elites has broken down and all that remains is a party-controlled police apparatus. Everything, Kershaw explains, was now

> ...subordinate to the way the charismatic führer regime was structured, and how it functioned, in its dying phase. Paradoxically, it was by this time charismatic rule without charisma. Hitler's mass charismatic appeal had long since dissolved, but the structures and mentalities of his charismatic rule lasted until his death in the bunker. The dominant elites, divided as they were, possessed neither the collective will nor the mechanisms of power to prevent Hitler taking Germany to total destruction.[27]

The last months of the Hitler regime seem to have been the exception that proves the rule. Fascism almost invariably involves traditional conservatism, the state machine, and the fascist movement working in harness – though in some cases, like Nazi Germany, with the fascist movement, or at least its bureaucratised security-apparatus, increasingly dominant. There are no Chinese walls here: no hard lines of separation such as divide class enemies. Instead, there is negotiation, compromise, getting along; there is the hybrid authoritarian state, with its party appendages, acting to smash democracy and the labour movement in the interests of capital.

## LEADERS AND STREET-FIGHTERS
Fascist leaders often have contempt for their followers; they
tend to regard them as a means to an end, and as a potential
liability, both on the road to power, and more especially once it
has been secured.

Fascism creates a mass movement of middle-class and
working-class people by claiming to be anti-elite, anti-Establishment, anti-system. The leaders tell their supporters they
are going to 'take back control' from big-business profiteers
and corrupt, self-serving politicians. The 'old gang' is to be
replaced by 'new men' who will uphold the interests of the
people.

A glance at the Nazi Party Programme of 1920 – almost certainly written by Adolf Hitler and Anton Drexler – is salutary. It
includes the following points:

- Abolition of unearned incomes
- Abolition of the slavery of interest
- Confiscation of all war profits
- Nationalisation of all monopoly corporations
- Profit-sharing in all large industries
- Break-up of big department stores in favour of small
  traders
- Abolition of ground rent and prohibition on speculation
  in land
- Common criminals, usurers, and profiteers to be pun-
  ished with death[28]

Had this programme been implemented, it would have
amounted to the overthrow of German capitalism – and to the
execution of all capitalists! Clearly, it was incompatible with
fascism's central aim – the creation of an autarchic national-
capitalist bloc under authoritarian rule – the achievement of
which depended on an alliance with traditional elites, big business, and state functionaries.

Inherent in fascism, therefore, is a contradiction between essence and appearance, that is, between the practice of the leadership in cutting deals with power, and the promises they make to the 'human dust' that constitutes their party. This contradiction, increasingly problematic as the fascist movement grows, is liable to explode when the leadership enters national government. At this moment, with the movement at its peak, expectations are at fever-pitch. Yet this is precisely the moment when the leadership must demonstrate to its conservative allies that it can be trusted to govern in the interests of the system.

The contradiction tends to be mediated in four ways. First, large numbers of party activists are found jobs in the state apparatus: a good proportion of the mass movement is thereby bureaucratised and bought off. Second, attacks are authorised on the scapegoats of fascist propaganda: it is the oppressed – not the speculators – who thus become the targets of thugs pumped up with anger and aggression. Third, these attacks, by driving some of the victims out of employment or out of business, create vacancies for party supporters. Fourth, the hardcore party 'radicals' – those intent on trying to implement the fascist programme at the expense of traditional elites – are either marginalised or eliminated.

The history of Nazi Germany illustrates all of these processes. By 1935, an estimated 60% of senior civil-servants were Nazi Party members. That same year, Hitler decreed that 10% of all vacancies at the lower and middle levels of the civil service should be filled by members who had joined before September 1930 (the occasion of the first big electoral breakthrough). Party members moving into state positions seem to have morphed into typical civil servants, as social historian Richard Grunberger describes:

> ...the self-image of quite a few Nazis who had obtained administrative posts in local government...underwent a characteristically German transformation: they tended to look upon themselves increasingly as state officials rather

than party functionaries, so that by 1935 nearly 40% of Nazi-appointed mayors and more than half the local councillors had become inactive in the party.[29]

At the same time, the accumulated energy of the movement was expressed in waves of officially sanctioned anti-semitic violence – notably, on a national scale, in 1933, 1935, and 1938. On each of these occasions, state legislation coincided with an upsurge of street thuggery. In spring 1933, the party first proclaimed a boycott of Jewish businesses and called for action committees to implement this, then legislated against Jews working as civil servants, lawyers, and doctors. In September 1935, the notorious 'Nuremberg Laws' were introduced, denying German citizenship to Jews and banning intermarriage and sexual intercourse with Gentiles. Then, in November 1938, came the *Kristallnacht* ('Crystal Night') pogrom. The number of Jewish-owned businesses had already fallen from 50,000 to 9,000, but the aim now was for 'Aryanisation' to be pushed to its logical conclusion: the elimination of the Jews from German economic life entirely. On the night of 9/10 November, mobs of SA Brownshirts went into action across Germany, burning 1,000 synagogues, wrecking 7,000 businesses, murdering at least 90 people, sending 30,000 to the concentration camps. Ian Kershaw, the biographer of Hitler, explains the logic of such pogroms:

> The party leaders were, in fact, reacting to and channelling pressures emanating from radicals at the grassroots of the movement. The continuing serious disaffection within the ranks of the SA...was the underlying impetus to the new wave of violence directed at the Jews. Feeling cheated of the brave new world they thought was theirs, alienated and demoralised, the toughs of the SA needed a new sense of purpose. As internal SA reports indicated, they were also more than spoiling for a fight with their ideological enemies – Jews, Catholics, and capitalists.[30]

Even so, the pressure-values – absorption into the state apparatus, the taking over of Jewish businesses, violent attacks on minorities – were barely adequate to manage the accumulated energy of the fascist mass-movement. Only the war – with its vastly expanded opportunities in the occupied territories – would permit its final dissipation. Long before then, the regime had been compelled to launch a ruthless attack on its own intractable 'radicals'. This was the internal Nazi Party coup known as 'the Night of the Long Knives'.

SA leader Ernst Röhm's demand for a 'second revolution' to redistribute wealth was worrying German capital and destabilising the state. So between 30 June and 2 July 1934, the SS carried out a series of extrajudicial executions, which included Röhm himself, other leading Nazi 'left-wingers', and various establishment conservatives and others opposed to the regime. At least 85 people were killed, possibly as many as 200, and the effect was decisive: the rowdy, brown-shirted thugs of the Nazi struggle for power were brought under control; the cold, disciplined, black-uniformed killers of the Nazi dictatorship – Heinrich Himmler's SS – emerged as the new party elite.[31]

## CONCLUSION

In the last two chapters, we have drawn on the historical experience of fascism in an effort to understand it. We have found it to be a mass political movement based on nationalism, racism, sexism, authoritarianism, and violence. We have also shown it to be a 'movement' in the most literal sense of a *process*. It varies in form from place to place and over time. It is shaped by the conjuncture in which it operates, that is, by its interaction and collision with other social forces in each concrete historical situation. Like a river, it is defined by motion itself.

We have also shown that, although fascism builds by accumulating the human detritus of capitalist crisis around a promise of radical change, it is in fact an irredeemably reactionary project. It is an ultra-conservative movement wholly committed to the capitalist system, one intent on the destruction of democracy, the unions, the social movements, and all forms of dissent and resistance.

But, as explained in this chapter, the contradiction between essence and appearance – between ultra-conservatism in purpose and radical promise in rhetoric – is a source of tension. Cutting deals with traditional elites, maintaining a façade of respectability, managing the violence inherent in the movement, these and other problems represent vulnerabilities. Fascist movements can be undermined and derailed – by mass movements of the working class that understand what they are about and act decisively while there is still time. This, too, is one of history's many lessons. As we shall see in Chapter 7, fascist movements have often gone down to defeat.

Before discussing anti-fascist activity, however, we must turn our attention to defining the threat we face today. History repeats itself, but never exactly. We can learn from the past, but we must apply the lessons to new circumstances. In the next chapter, therefore, we assess the compound crisis of modern capitalism in its economic, social, and political dimensions – the context for what we are calling 'creeping fascism' – and in Chapter 5 we analyse the growing movements of the Far Right in Europe and the United States today.

## CHAPTER 4

# The world crisis

What might be called 'classical fascism' arose in the context of an interwar crisis of economic collapse, social dislocation, and political polarisation. Our argument is that what we face today is 'creeping fascism' in the context of another systemic crisis.

We begin our story with a flashback to 2008. *Newsnight* economist Paul Mason described the global banking crash of that year as 'the greatest man-made economic catastrophe in human history'. We have been living with the consequences ever since: we have been living in the epoch of neoliberal austerity.

In September 2007, the so-called 'credit crunch' turned critical when the British building society Northern Rock went bust. Exactly a year later, the giant US investment bank Lehman Brothers announced astronomical losses of $3.9 billion and declared itself bankrupt.

On 18 September 2008, fearing a chain reaction of bank failures, Ben Bernanke, head of the US central bank, and Henry Paulson, US finance minister, announced that 'We are headed for the worst financial crisis in the nation's history. We're talking about a matter of days.'

To prevent this, world rulers ripped up their free-market textbooks and carried out a series of monster nationalisations and bailouts. Almost immediately, a global total of around $2 trillion of state funding was injected into the banks, two-thirds in direct spending, one-third in the form of guarantees.

Since then, trillions more have been handed over. One estimate of US government spending on bailouts between 2008 and 2012 put the total at $30 trillion.

The pumping of unprecedented amounts of state capital into private banks stabilised the global financial system. It covered immediate losses, and, more importantly, restored 'confidence' by demonstrating to finance-capitalists that the state would not allow major banks to fail. Profits remained private, but losses would be 'nationalised'. Speculators continued to sweep up the winning chips, but taxpayers would henceforward cover the bad bets.

This has not solved the crisis; it has merely reconfigured it. The 2008 Crash, unprecedented in scale, has shrunk the financial reserves of states, corporations, and households, and pitched the world economy into slump.

The state funds shovelled into the banks have simply disappeared into a black hole of bad debt. Since 2008, moreover, the rich have been getting richer even faster than before. The casino-economy is again in full swing. The next bubble is inflating fast. The world seems on the brink of another crash.

Across the world, bailouts for the rich have meant austerity for the rest. The real economy is mired in long-term stagnation. Instead of investment for human need and a green transition, we have an economy based on debt, speculation, and the further enrichment of the 1%.

The austerity and stagnation of a busted economic model are fuelling a wider crisis of the global system as a whole. Inequality and injustice are tearing apart the social fabric. The international order is breaking down. War has engulfed entire societies and displaced tens of millions. Fascists and racists are gaining ground. Democracy is being hollowed out and civil liberties eroded. Global warming threatens the planet and the whole of humanity with climate catastrophe.

These problems are connected. They are all aspects of a single compound crisis of neoliberal capitalism – or of what we call here, in more technical language, 'global financialised monopoly-capitalism'.

This chapter focuses on three aspects of that compound crisis. This does not mean that we regard other aspects – like imperialist war and climate catastrophe – as unimportant. It simply means that these are the three aspects that we must focus on to contextualise the rise of the Far Right. So we concentrate here on the economic, social, and political aspects of the crisis as they are playing out in Europe and the United States.

## THE BUBBLE ECONOMY

We have arrived at an impasse in human history.[1] Capitalism entered the fifth phase of its existence – 'neoliberal capitalism' – in the 1970s. This, like the preceding phases of mercantile, industrial, imperial, and state-managed capitalism, can be defined as a stage in an ongoing process of 'centralisation and concentration of capital', whereby the average unit of capital becomes steadily larger. Periodically, this incremental *quantitative* development gives rise to abrupt shifts in the *qualitative* character of the system. The system in its current neoliberal phase can be defined as 'global financialised monopoly-capitalism'.

Let us unpack this term. Global in the sense that the major corporations have burst their national shells and are operating as transnational or multinational units of capital. The relative economic power of the nation-state has, in consequence, been drastically reduced. Nowadays, instead of states regulating capital, capital dictates to states.

Financialised in the sense that the dominant circuit of capital is no longer the industrial/productive circuit, but a financial/parasitic circuit. In the former, capital is invested in raw materials, energy, machinery, and labour-power to produce goods and services which are then marketed to earn profit. In the latter, capital is invested in property or monetary assets, and profit is taken either in the form of rent or interest, or in the form of speculative gains when asset is sold on at a higher price.[2]

In other words, most capital investment in the modern economy does not result in an increasing flow of goods and services, since, in the now-dominant financial circuit, nothing is produced, no social purpose is served, and no-one is better-off except for the speculators, who, in trading in monetary assets, gambling with electronic money, inflating a succession of asset-price bubbles, succeed in altering the distribution of claims on real wealth in their own favour.

The modern economy, in short, is *primarily* a debt economy. Debt – credit money created in the computer circuitry of private banks – is the main commodity being traded on today's global markets. The bulk of the debt relates to real estate – around two-thirds of the total on some estimates – and most of the real estate in question takes the form of already existing assets: in other words, it is not funding construction of new buildings, so much as the buying and selling of existing buildings with the effect of driving up prices.

The last part of our definition of the system – that it is a form of monopoly-capitalism – is directly related to the rise of the debt economy. Modern capitalism is not 'free market'. Handfuls of giant corporations dominate each sector of the global market, giving them the power to act as market-managers and price-makers. Competition is a secondary feature of the system. It has little impact on prices, since the corporate giants collaborate to organise markets and fix prices. It is primarily a matter of branding, packaging, advertising, upgrades, redesigns, and so on; it is concerned with seducing and bamboozling consumers, not providing them with good value.

The reconfiguring of competition has major consequences for the dynamics of the system. Corporations are inherently risk-averse. They crave stability, certainty, guaranteed sales and profits. In the mid 19th century, however, when many small firms competed, business-owners had no choice but to innovate, invest, and strive to reduce prices by using labour-saving technology. In the last 150 years or so, the rise of monopoly has made the system increasingly sluggish and stagnant, as competitive pressure reduces, the cost of global-level investment rises, and corporate managements seeks easier, quicker, safer profit in other ways. The consequent shift from the industrial circuit to the financial circuit reached a tipping-point in the 1970s. In a sense, the 'neoliberal counter-revolution' spearheaded by Thatcher in Britain and Reagan in the States and then rolled out across the world economy was the political expression of this transition.

The implications are profound. The world is saddled with an economic system characterised by deep-rooted underlying stagnation-slump, an overblown, unstable, and parasitic financial infrastructure, and grotesque and fast-growing social inequality. It is also a system of anarchic growth, beyond democratic control, without rational plan or social purpose, that now endangers the survival of the planetary ecosystem.

The system is irredeemably flawed at the level of its basic laws of motion. It cannot be reformed. To rescue humanity and save the planet, we have to halt the entire process of financialised capital-accumulation. We have to terminate the debt economy, and establish collective democratic control over economic life.

This, however, turns out to be a problem of awesome historic difficulty. That the world is in crisis goes unquestioned on any part of the political spectrum. That the root cause is a highly dysfunctional economic system is widely accepted among a swathe of the more intelligent commentators on both the left *and the right*. Consider this example: 'We need to ask why debt contracts exist, what benefits they bring, and what risks they inevitably create. We need to question whether banks should exist at all.'

Who wrote this? A Marxist revolutionary? A radical Keynesian economist? No: these words, and many more like them, appear in Adair Turner's new book *Between Debt and the Devil*.

Turner, a top banker, is so much an insider, so much part of the global financial elite, that his willingness to challenge the neoliberal consensus head-on is a remarkable testimony to his

intelligence and integrity. He served as Director of the Confedera-
tion of British Industry in the late 1990s, and was then appointed
Chairman of the Financial Services Authority just as the global
financial crisis struck. His honesty is disarming: he entitles the
preface to his new book 'The crisis I didn't see coming'. He now
condemns modern capitalism for uncontrolled credit creation
without social purpose, for the gargantuan waste of its real-estate
bubbles, for lumbering the global economy with a crushing debt
overhang, and for hoovering wealth to the top of society.

Yet the entire political establishment – from traditional conservatives to social-democrats – continues to mouth neoliberal
mantras and impose the austerity demanded by the bankers.
No-one has the vision or the courage to propose an alternative
economy strategy appropriate to the scale and character of the
crisis. Everyone collaborates to prop up a bankrupt system by
bailing out the rich and dumping on the poor.

This is the democratic deficit at work. The glaring failures
of the system seem to be beyond any effective political challenge. How come?

Some of the more insightful and socially concerned members of the global elite understand the predicament they are
in. This we have acknowledged. They know that the financial
system is loaded with debt, austerity has deflated demand, and
the real economy is stagnant. They know that nothing is working:
none of the policy levers on which they pull – low interest rates,
quantitative easing, tax cuts for corporations – is regenerating
the economy. Instead, the combination of deleveraging (paying
down debt) and austerity (cuts in benefits, wages, and public services) have collapsed demand. So there is no incentive for firms
to invest in the real economy, and every incentive for them to
invest in the get-rich-quick money and real-estate markets.

Turner has the figures: 'On average, in advanced economies,
public debt increased by 34% of GDP between 2007 and 2014.'
The debt economy, in other words, has surged *since* the Crash.

The success of the rich in continuing to accumulate wealth

since 2008 is truly awesome. An Oxfam study found that the richest 388 people owned the same as the poorest 50% of the world's population (3.5 billion people) in 2010. Four years later, just 85 people had this much wealth. Now, it is down to eight.

The occupants of a golf buggy, in other words, have the same wealth us half of humanity. The same study revealed that the richest 1% – the world's ruling class as a whole – control more wealth than all the rest of us combined. This wealth, of course, is hoarded in tax havens, out of reach of government taxation.

At the base of the debt economy is the working class. As discussed in Chapter 2, an intermediate layer of administrators, managers, higher professionals, and business people exists beneath the 1%, enjoying relative social privilege as the reward for their role in organising and policing the process of exploitation by which wealth is hoovered upwards. Below them stands the working class, which comprises up to 90% of the population. It includes factory workers, nurses, sales assistants, teachers, train drivers, call-centre workers, local government officers, electricians, care workers, junior civil servants, hospital porters, fast-food workers, and many more. We consider them all to be part of one social class.

We explained in Chapter 2 why we take this view: it is because they all engage in collective labour to create wealth – an economic process; and because they are all exploited, both as workers and consumers, by the 1%, who live off the surplus created by their labour – a social relationship. Here is how it works in what we are calling 'the permanent debt economy'.

First, the rate of exploitation 'at the point of production' – that is, in the workplaces – has increased substantially in the neoliberal era, with the weakening of union organisation and the atomisation of the workforce. The change is reflected in the proliferation of low-wage/no prospects 'McJobs', part-time working, temporary contracts, zero-hours contracts, compulsory 'self-employment', and other exploitative labour-practices of the so-called 'gig economy'. Capital favours a casualised labour-force – their word for it is 'flexible' – because it weakens the unions and keeps wages low.

Second, in this era of financialisation, the rate of exploitation 'at the point of consumption' has shot up. It takes the form of excessive rents and mortgage payments on overpriced housing, ever-rising transport costs, extortionate utility charges, rip-off prices in the shops, credit-card debts, Wonga debts, and more. In Britain, for example, the current estimate (at the time of writing) for total unsecured credit stands at £192 billion, while that for average household debt (*excluding* mortgages) stands at £12,000.[3]

Third, there is the rampant plundering of 'the commons' by private capital, as public services are privatised or 'contracted out' for the sole purpose of creating new revenue streams for corporate profiteers. Take the slow strangulation (by funding cuts) and dismemberment (by privatisation) of Britain's NHS. It is a process of deliberate destruction by the political and corporate elite of what was perhaps the finest and fairest healthcare system in the world. The reason? Leading Tories have been speaking for years about the NHS as 'Britain's biggest enterprise'. They have been bragging about their intention to open up the £100 billion a year NHS oyster to private profit.

And the profits are indeed immense. The current debt crisis in the NHS is largely a result of the PFI (Private Finance Initiative) schemes imposed on the service as a way of building new hospitals. The cost of these projects over 25 years is expected to be *six times* the value of the actual infrastructure.[4] The source of this revenue stream is, of course, working-class income – taken in the form of tax revenues and paid in the form of interest on government debt.

In the end, the reason the banks are bailed out, the NHS privatised, and the poor squeezed is very simple: it makes the rich richer. The financial circuit of capital is now the primary mechanism by which the rich grow richer at the expense of the rest of society. Financialised capitalism, backed by state power,

is siphoning wealth from the productive 90% to the parasitic 1%. The life-blood of society is being sucked out by the
pointless vampire-like existence of the super-rich. That is the
inner essence of the debt economy and of global financialised
monopoly-capitalism in the early 21$^{st}$ century.

What is happening is both economically insane and socially
indefensible. Demand is being sucked out of the economy. The
commanding heights are dominated by giant corporations
that sit on vast cash-piles they refuse to invest productively.
Wages stagnate and debts mount for millions of working-class
households. Mass unemployment is permanent, but welfare is
cut and poverty increases. Public services decay as they are
starved of funds or sold off. Only the rich benefit: they just get
richer and richer.

Yet in the face of this, the greatest economic crisis since the
1930s, the political elite does nothing. It appears demoralised,
drifting, without ideas or solutions, unable to act, evoking contempt and derision. Here, for example, is how a *Guardian* report
described the Euro-elite at the beginning of 2017, as the tide of
nationalism and racism rose all around them:

> A few weeks ago, a significant anniversary in Maastricht
> slipped by almost unnoticed: 25 years ago, the historic
> treaty that ushered in the euro was drafted. But there was
> no fanfare, no commemoration in the European Parlia-
> ment, no mention by the Commission. There was just a
> rather lacklustre speech by Jean-Claude Juncker...
>
> This air of resignation perfectly epitomises an EU in
> retreat. Battered on all sides by crises – Brexit, the euro,
> refugees – the Union is short of ideas, perhaps shorter
> than it has ever been...
>
> One clear lesson of 2016 was that right-wing pop-
> ulism seemed to appeal to voters because it, at least, had
> ideas. On the other hand, the message from nation-states
> is overwhelmingly one of 'less Europe'.

>   And so Europe is paralysed, torn between putting
>   forward ideas that can hit back against demagogues, and
>   restraining its own meddling tendencies.[5]

The old order is dead, but not buried. A bankrupt economic system is leeching the life-blood out of society. Grotesque greed runs rampant at the top, while austerity and squalor destroy the foundations. And the political elite – corrupt, complacent, devoid of imagination or will – does nothing. This is the economic preparation for fascism.

## THE HOLLOW SOCIETY

In 1958, the American liberal economist John Kenneth Galbraith published a book, *The Affluent Society*, in which be bemoaned the coincidence of 'private affluence and public squalor'. An advocate of Keynesian-type state intervention and welfare provision, his theme was the insidious idea that private profit was good and public service bad; an idea reflected in the contrast between a booming 'consumer society' which everyone at the time seemed to approve, and the churlish reluctance with which government funding was dribbled into public infrastructure and social provision.

The post-war boom, which lasted until 1973, masked the relative backwardness of the public sector. In many countries, not least in Britain, expenditure on public housing, health care, education, social services, and welfare payments was rising. Debate centred not on 'cuts', but on the priorities for new outlays. Unions were strong, living standards were rising, social inequalities were reducing, and 'the welfare state' was a matter of broad consensus.

But in 1973, the world economy was plunged into a new crisis – one from which it has never fully recovered. The growth rate in the US economy, which had been 5.9% during the Second World War and 4.4% during the post-war boom, slumped to 3.1% during the 1980s and 1990s, and has been bumping along at around 2.6% in the years since.[6] It is this underlying sickness in the system – its running down into permanent stagnation-slump – that triggered 'the neoliberal counter-revolution'.

During the 1970s, an alternative to the 'state-capitalist' model of economic development gained support among some mainstream politicians. In the 1980s, neoliberalism became the basis of government policy under Margaret Thatcher in Britain and Ronald Reagan in the US. After that, especially in the wake of the 1989 revolutions against the Stalinist dictatorships in Eastern Europe, the new model was rolled out across the world.

Neoliberalism was a response to the problem of low profits and sluggish growth. It involved a frontal assault on unions, wages, and the welfare state. The aim was to redistribute wealth from labour to capital. Higher profit, argued Thatcher and Reagan, would encourage enterprise, investment, and growth.

The rulers of the world were, in fact, launching a class war against working people in the interests of profit and wealth. The most decisive battle in that war was fought in Britain in 1984.

The previous Tory government had been broken by industrial action in 1972 and 1974. Thatcher was determined to mount a full-scale counterattack against the unions, the public sector, and the working class. The miners were the most important target. They had spearheaded the struggle against the previous Tory administration.

A massive programme of pit closures provoked the miners into a desperate battle to save their livelihoods and communities. It turned into the longest mass strike in history – 150,000 men on strike for a year (1984-85). The miners faced paramilitary police violence, courtroom frame-ups, and a barrage of media lies. They were eventually starved back to work.

The defeat of the miners broke the back of British trade unionism. In the early 1970s, the British working class was one of the best organised and most militant in the world. Since 1985 union membership has halved, and over the last 25 years the British strike rate has been lower than at any time since the 19th century.

It is now clear that the defeat of the British miners had global significance: it was the single most important break-through in the international ruling class's attempt to smash working-class resistance to neoliberalism.

Most immediately, it enabled Thatcher and her successors in Britain to unroll a programme of cuts and sell-offs. The main beneficiaries have been the super-rich and the global mega-corporations of neoliberal capitalism.

The most straightforward measure of the success of the ruling-class offensive is the huge increase in social inequality across the globe since the 1970s. In this respect, the neoliberals have succeeded in reversing all of the gains of the last century.

The pay of top CEOs (chief executive officers) in the US, for example, increased by 1000% between 1978 and 2014, while workers' wages averaged just 11% increases. This meant that, whereas in 1965 CEOs had been paid only 20 times as much as their workers, they were now earning more than 300 times as much.[7]

This, as Thomas Piketty has explained, is less a matter of Adam Smith's 'invisible hand' than of 'hands in the till' on the part of a corporate elite whose greed is now beyond any form of social control.[8] Nor are grotesquely inflated salaries their only source of income. The higher up their ranks you go, the greater the proportion of income the elite derive from revenues generated by capital ownership, rising to 60% among the top 0.01% of the population.[9] The surging of private capital is, in fact, a primary economic tendency of the neoliberal era, its value relative to national income doubling in the rich countries between 1970 and 2010.[10]

The opposite process operates at the base of the system: the mass of the population is getting poorer relative to the top echelon. On a rough estimate, the labour/capital division of national wealth was probably around two-thirds/one-third in the 1970s, whereas now it is around half and half.

In the United States, though the official unemployment rate

is only 5%, real wages have barely budged for decades. The living standards of American workers have been static or falling since the 1970s. The $4 an hour average of private-sector workers in 1973 represented more purchasing power than today's $21 average. Some 43 million Americans – one in six – are officially classed as living in poverty.[11]

This is the failed 'American Dream', the end of the 'Good Society', the collapse of the post-war 'welfare' consensus. It is the social base for the rise of the Far Right. The *Guardian*'s Gary Younge, covering the US presidential election from the rustbelt town of Muncie, Indiana, summed up the way in which Trump's racism connected with social despair:

> [The] sense of racial fragility was both local and global, real and imaginary. At home, white people will become a minority in around 25 years, the president is the black child of a mixed-race relationship that involved a lapsed foreign Muslim, the southern border is porous, and black people are on the streets again, demanding equality before the law. Abroad, jihadi terrorists are becoming ever more brazen and brutal in their attacks on western cities and civilians, the Chinese economy will soon be larger than America's, the US military has failed to deliver victory in several Muslim countries, and refugees are desperately fleeing the Middle East. Add all that to the stagnant wages, falling living-standards, decreasing life-expectancy, and vanishing class-mobility, and you can see how being a white American feels like it's not what it used to be.[12]

Younge's article captures the pervading sense of malaise, drift, and hopelessness that goes beyond the immediate pain of poverty. More academic studies have come to similar conclusions about the social base of the Far Right.

The authors of a Joseph Rowntree Foundation survey

of voting behaviour in the British EU referendum concluded that, while poverty mattered, so did place, with people living in districts afflicted with social decay and restricted opportunities more likely to vote Leave irrespective of their own circumstances. 'A geographic divide overlays the social divide,' the authors concluded.

> Even if people possess educational qualifications and skills, if they are stuck in left-behind areas that are experiencing decline, then they are less likely to be presented with local opportunities to use these skills and get ahead in life. Such an environment can fuel feelings of exclusion or marginalisation.[13]

As Richard Wilkinson and Kate Pickett have demonstrated so well in *The Spirit Level*, inequality corrodes the social fabric as a whole. It eats away at any general sense of well-being, and leaves individuals feeling disconnected and marginalised. The authors found that almost all social problems were more common in more unequal societies – regardless of the overall level of wealth. So, for example, in more unequal societies like the US, Britain, Portugal, and New Zealand, the level of homicides, mental illness, teenage pregnancies, and so on were much higher than in more equal societies like Norway, Sweden, Finland, Denmark, and Japan.[14]

We want to pursue this further by reference to the concept of 'civil society'. A short historical digression may help.

The epoch between 1875 and 1914 saw the spread of democracy, the rise of labour, and an explosive development of 'civil society' across Europe and the United States.[15] A strong civil society remained characteristic of the interwar period. Perhaps, in Britain at least, it culminated in the Second World War, in what Angus Calder in his classic study of the British Home Front between 1939 and 1945 called 'the people's war'.[16]

By civil society we mean neither the formal state at one

extreme nor the private household at the other, but the entire network of public institutions and activities, political, social, and cultural, which cause people to come together in groups for common purpose; everything from a local sports club to a national trade union. When civil society is dense and large numbers engage in collective activity, the effect is to foster a sense of joint endeavour, of community and solidarity, of caring and sharing. Let us illustrate this with two snapshots.

The growth of European capitalism from the 1870s onwards had created an industrial working class of tens of millions by 1914. Mass strikes had welded this working class into a combative labour movement across much of Europe and the United States. This in turn had created an electoral base for mass socialist parties like the German Social-Democratic Party (SPD). By 1912, with a million members and 90 daily papers, the SPD was the biggest working class organisation in the world. It ran a women's section, a youth section, various trade unions and co-ops, and numerous sports clubs and cultural societies.[17] It amounted to a radical 'counter-cultural' alternative to German conservatism and liberalism, one in which a distinct working-class identity founded on resistance to the bosses and the state was fostered.

Or take the situation in Britain in the late 1930s. The labour movement was at a low ebb following the defeat of a general strike, the collapse of a Labour government, and unprecedented levels of unemployment. But when left-wing publisher Victor Gollancz launched the Left Book Club in May 1936, it gained 6,000 members in its first month and 40,000 members by the end of the year. At its peak, in 1939, its membership hit 57,000, it had distributed 2 million books, and there were around 1,200 local groups. These included geographical, occupational, and workplace groups, and they engaged in a wide range of cultural and political activities, including public meetings, film showings, theatre productions, solidarity work (e.g. with Spain), political agitation (e.g. against appeasement), and much else.[18]

This strong civil-society tradition underpinned the British war effort, notably during the Blitz, when an estimated one million Londoners were enrolled in some form of 'civil defence' work, prompting the Yorkshire radical J B Priestley to suggest on the radio in 1940 that Britain was finally being 'bombed and burned into democracy'.[19]

We inhabit a very different world. Civil society has been hollowed out. Public institutions have become shrunken and ossified. The unions fail to recruit new workers or to mount effective resistance to rapacious employers. The socialist parties have alienated their supporters by morphing into election machines run by technocratic careerists. The mass of the people have retreated from the social arena into a closed world of privatised consumption. Society has become atomised, alienated, and anomic (linked concepts to which we will return below).

The most glaring change, and the one with the most serious political implications, is the decline of the labour movement. This seems to be a world-wide phenomenon, reflected in falling union membership, falling strike rates, falling membership of social-democratic parties, and falling support for such parties at the ballot box.

Union membership has fallen almost everywhere, in some cases only modestly, but in many precipitously, dropping to a half or even a third of peak levels during the neoliberal era. In the United States, the drop is from nearly one in three unionised to barely one in ten; in Britain, from 13 million to only 6.5 million; in France, from 18% to just 8%.

But this is not an adequate measure of the damage to organised labour. These figures conceal a deeper collapse in workplace organisation and industrial militancy. The US, for example, experienced hundreds of major labour-disputes each year between the early 1950s and the late 1970s. At that point, the strike rate plunged downwards, until a dozen a year was normal. This meant that, whereas in 1952 roughly 4.5% of the entire civilian labour force had taken some sort of industrial action that year, by 2013 it was a mere 0.04%. The picture was similar in Britain, where the strike rate collapsed from a peak of 29.5 million days in 1979 to just 0.7 million days under the Major and Blair governments.

Underlying these shifts is a change in both workplace union organisation and the nature of strike action. In the 1970s, union members were often involved in electing work-place reps, attending union meetings, taking part in unofficial or 'wildcat' action – in other words, their union membership meant face-to-face collective organisation and sometimes action. Nowadays, union membership tends to be a matter of individual case-work, political lobbying, and the occasional one-day strike. The shop-steward has been replaced by the union lawyer, the mass meeting by the head-office email, the all-out strike by the token protest. The unions have become less organs of mass struggle from below, and more lobbyists and suppliers of services to members.

This is what we mean by 'the hollow society'. It is one in which the civil-society institutions that bring people together – to engage, to organise, to resist, to fight – have atrophied. This does not mean an absence of protest. On the contrary: recent years have seen street protests of unprecedented size on a wide range of issues – against war, austerity, racism, climate catastrophe, dictatorship, capitalism. We will discuss the significance of these events in Chapter 7. Our point here is that, whatever the significance and potential of mass street-protest, recent social movements – unlike the great protest movements of the past – have not been rooted in strong civil-society structures able to sustain and amplify them. They have had a lamentable tendency to rise like rockets and fall like sticks. The hollow society abounds with spontaneity, but lacks ballast. Politics, in consequence, seems to take place in a kind of void.

## THE POLITICAL VOID

Disempowerment is demoralising. The decline of the labour movement and of civil society more generally has left people atomised and vulnerable in the face of power. Politicians evolve into careerists and technocrats without a social base. Public services are turned into corporate enterprises. Work is casualised, hours are increased, terms and conditions get worse, pay stagnates. Bullying, stress, and fear dominate the workplace. This neoliberal dystopia of corporate power, atomised workers, and privatised consumption is a world of abiding alienation.

Without a strong public power – without the collective strength of organised labour – private interests run rampant, and corruption, greed, and selfishness dominate the social realm. People, despite their powerlessness, sense it. Confidence in politicians, political parties, the mass media, the police, the banks is down everywhere. In Britain, trust in banks collapsed from 90% in 1983 to 19% in 2012.[20] Across Europe, only 48% 'tend to trust' the broadcast media, and only 43% the written media.[21] In the United States, those expressing 'a great deal' or 'quite a lot' of confidence in the presidency are down to 36%, in the criminal justice system 23%, and in Congress a paltry 9%.[22] There is a crisis of confidence in the central institutions of modern liberal-democratic societies.

The process of decay is self-reinforcing. The weakening of the labour movement and of civil society more generally leads to disempowerment and disengagement as citizens retreat into a privatised world of individual household consumption. This means that the public realm is left almost entirely to corporate capital and the state apparatus. Greed and corruption are therefore less constrained. With democracy in retreat, graft flourishes. This confirms the impression that all politicians are 'the same' and 'out for themselves'. Cynicism deepens the sense of alienation from 'the system'.

The much-vaunted 'democratic deficit' is thus a two-sided process. On the one hand, the political elite is increasingly remote and unrepresentative; on the other, the masses are increasingly withdrawn from the political process. This contradiction is a massive crisis for liberal parliamentary democracy. If the political and corporate elite is out of control and the electorate is too alienated and disengaged to rein it in, then the political system is broken. We have, in short, the 'de-politicisation' of politics and the 'de-democratisation' of democracy.

A further problem is that a growing number of decisions are made by non-democratic institutions like the IMF, the EU, the central banks, the big corporations, and so on – a consequence of both globalisation and the decline of the international labour movement.

Elected politicians make fewer important decisions than ever, and, in any case, the parties have converged in a pro-corporate, pro-finance, pro-market consensus that reduces the differences between them to matters of style rather than substance. Instead of public debates about principles and policies, electors are invited to choose between rival teams of celebrities and technocrats. It would be a politics of spectacle – or perhaps of soap opera – were it not so crushingly dull. The nosediving of party membership and voter turnout tells us all we need to know.

In 13 of Europe's established democracies, party membership fell between 1980 and 2009 by anything from 27% (in Germany) to 66% (in Britain); the only exceptions to the general trend were Spain, Greece, and Portugal. This is paralleled by steady falls in the number of people identifying strongly, or at all, with one particular party ('party loyalists'), and steady falls in overall voter turnout in general elections, with 80%, even 90%, turnouts common between 1945 and the 1980s, but with figures plummeting in the neoliberal era, to 75% in Italy in 2013, 71% in Germany the same year, 66% in Britain in 2015, and 55% in France in 2012.[23]

Levels of participation have always been far lower in the United States, probably in large part because of the absence of a mass social-democratic party able to enthuse working-class voters. Even here, though, the contemporary political malaise is evident. In 2015, only 43% of Americans had a favourable opinion of the Democratic Party, and even fewer, 38%, of the Republican Party. In the 2016 presidential election, only 43% were 'very or fairly satisfied' with the Democratic candidate (Hillary Clinton), and only 40% with the Republican candidate (Donald Trump).[24]

The conclusion drawn by the late Peter Mair, author of *Ruling the Void*, was gloomy. His sense was that 'the age of party democracy' had passed, and that parties had become 'so disconnected from the wider society, and pursue a form of competition that is so lacking in meaning, that they no longer seem capable of sustaining democracy in its present form'.[25]

> The last decades of the 20th century witnessed a gradual but also inexorable withdrawal of the parties from the realm of civil society towards the realm of government and the state, and together, these two processes have led to a situation in which each party tends to become more distant from the voters that it purports to represent, while at the same time tending to become more closely associated with the alternative protagonists against which it purports to compete.[26]

Mair locates this crisis of representative democracy firmly in the context of the long-term decay of civil society. Classic social-democratic parties were based on strong unions. Classic faith-based parties were based on strong churches. Classic conservative parties were based on upper-class networks, business associations, and farmers groups. Political organisations were part of

> a generalised pattern of social and political segmentation that helped root parties in the society and to stabilise and distinguish their electorates... With the

increasing individualisation of society, traditional collective identities and organisational affiliations count
for less, including those that once formed part of party-
centred networks.[27]

Detached from civil society and evolving into part of the
state, parties have ceased to be 'representative' and become
instead 'procedural'. No longer society's representative in government, the neoliberalised party of the contemporary political
system has become 'the government's representative in society'. Instead of politicians fighting to implement democratic
mandates in the interests of ordinary voters, they have become
professional habitués of the remote realm of state officialdom:
no longer 'one of us', they are now 'one of them'.[28]

## CONCLUSION

Without unions to defend them or parties to represent them,
the mass of working people find themselves adrift in a neoliberal dystopia of corporate power. We define the human experience of this dystopia in terms of three overlapping concepts:
atomisation, alienation, and anomie.

Atomisation arises when the collectives of a strong civil
society – most importantly, the unions and socialist parties
that form the labour movement – are shattered, leaving individual workers at the mercy of their employers and more likely
to spend their leisure time in privatised consumption than in
public activity. This, from the perspective of capital, is the ideal:
a world of atomised workers whose wages can be driven down,
and of privatised consumers paying inflated prices for things
they do not need, extortionate charges for things they do need,
and interest on debts they wish they did not have.

Our understanding of alienation is rooted in our sense that
human beings have certain needs – biological, emotional, intellectual – the satisfaction of which allows them to be happy and
healthy, the frustration of which makes them unhappy and ill. And

since we are social animals, all our needs depend upon others, so that neoliberal capitalism's assault on families, communities, and unions is an assault on the fabric of social wellbeing. The root of alienation is the sundering of human bonds and of the possibilities inherent in such bonds for achieving fulfilment in love, sociability, creativity, collective labour, and making a social contribution.

Atomisation and alienation violate our 'species-being', our essential human nature, as shaped by a distinct set of biologically and culturally determined needs. They also dissolve the social frameworks within which positive norms and values develop – the norms and values upon which the individual's sense of identity, role, and self-respect to a large degree depend. De-anchored, the isolated individual of modern society, the lonely soul of the neoliberal dystopia, finds herself stranded in a moral vacuum. The wider world is a place of competition, exploitation, and impersonal, instrumental, 'what's-in-it-for-me' interactions. It is a place of bureaucratic indifference, of computer-generated responses, and of remote, unreachable, incomprehensible 'authority'. It is a place devoid of socially affirmative norms and values – a place of 'anomie' or normlessness.

We have defined the contemporary neoliberal world in terms of the bubble economy, the hollow society, and the political void. We describe the human experience of this world as one of atomisation, alienation, and anomie. And we find it unsurprising, in the light of this, that we seem to be facing an epidemic of mass psychotic rage.

This, we argue, is the context for fascism's 'second wave'. To this – the mass movements of the Far Right today – we now turn.

# CHAPTER 5
# The Far Right today

A far-right government has taken power in the United States. Far-right governments also hold power in Poland and Hungary. The leader of Austria's far-right Freedom Party came within a whisker of becoming national president. Far-right parties are mass electoral formations holding second or third place in the polls in about half the countries of Europe.[1]

These parties have infected the entire mainstream political spectrum with racism. Traditional conservative, liberal, and social-democratic parties are responding to a haemorrhaging of votes by echoing the anti-migrant and Islamophobic rhetoric of the Far Right. This reinforces the racist discourse, strengthens its most extreme proponents, and further undermines the electoral stability of mainstream parties: a vicious spiral.

Some far-right parties are advancing directly on state power in their own right. Others are actual or *de facto* coalition partners, using their lodgement in the political system to gain leverage for their racism. Even where far-right parties do not as yet exercise any governmental power, their presence is reconfiguring the political landscape, creating terrain that affords them maximum traction for the next advance. The space for the development of more racist, more authoritarian, and more violent forms of fascism steadily expands.

In this chapter, we set out to survey this new terrain of the Far Right. To avoid either an arbitrary selection of countries for detailed discussion or a tedious catalogue of them all in turn, we have opted for some broad generalisations (at the risk of obscuring significant national differences), and we provide a summary table listing all the major far-right parties, their current support, and what they stand for, in an appendix. More detailed information about the far-right parties in each country can, of course, be found online, and we hope in due course to publish more of our own material in this way.

## FROM NEOLIBERALISM TO NATIONAL-SOCIALISM

The modern Far Right has two main roots. One extends back to the classical fascism of the interwar period, a tradition nursed through the lean years of the post-war boom by fringe fanatics and never wholly extinguished. It is usually possible to trace a line of connection through the careers of individual activists and through the myriad small groups as they formed, split, dissolved, and re-emerged under new names during the years between the late 1940s and the early 1970s. An especially clear example is Italy's *Movimento Sociale Italiano* (MSI), a direct descendant of Mussolini's Fascist Party in the immediate post-war period, from which the cleaned-up 'post-fascist' *Alleanza Nazionale* (AN) of Gianfranco Fini emerged in 1994. Within a decade, the AN was in the mainstream, forming part of various coalition governments under Silvio Berlusconi in the 2000s.

The other root is what we might call 'radical neoliberalism' – an extreme expression of the dominant free-market ideology of the last 35 years. In Britain, for example, where the neoliberal counter-revolution was pioneered under Thatcher, the Tory Right has always included a fringe of free-market 'ultras' whose economic views are indistinguishable from those of UKIP (though this may be set to change if, as seems possible, UKIP makes a populist/national-socialist turn under its new leadership). Five Tory ultras published a book called *Britannia Unchained: global lessons for growth and prosperity* in 2012, which, in Phil Hearse's words, 'is dripping with vicious right-wing class hatred and a demand finally to end the post-war settlement which gave workers a welfare state and employment rights'. For instance, the authors inform us that

> The British are among the worst idlers in the world. We work among the lowest hours, we retire early, and our productivity is poor. Whereas Indian children aspire to be doctors or businessmen, the British are more interested in football and pop music.[2]

That garbage like this can find a publisher tells us something about the level to which mainstream political discourse has descended in modern Britain. But the purpose is clear: the authors propose an extreme radicalisation of the neoliberal counter-revolution to destroy all remnants of the post-war settlement and reduce British workers to the level of the most exploited in the globalised economy. This places them alongside Nigel Farage, the smarmy millionaire stockbroker who has made a career out of posing as a 'man of the people' with fag, pint, and racist sound-bite. UKIP, best known for its anti-EU and anti-immigration stance, has also been, until now at least, a party of neoliberal extremists.

Classical fascism and ultra neoliberalism are, then, the twin roots of the modern Far Right. To a degree, these two traditions have been synthesised, but the relationship has often been an awkward one. Now, it seems, there is a shift – from neoliberalism to national-socialism.

We can define national-socialism as a combination of (real) economic nationalism and (rhetorical) social welfarism. Before exploring this shift in a little more detail, let us identify the factors responsible. The neoliberal counter-revolution has failed economically, with growth rates since the 1970s well below those of the post-war boom, and, in the eight years since the 2008 Crash, lower still. We are trapped in an intractable crisis of stagnation-slump, with permanent mass unemployment, static or falling living-standards for the majority, and decaying public services. The result is intensified competition in global markets and growing social discontent at home. This is driving a right-wing political turn away from globalisation towards protectionism and racism. It is summed up by Marine Le Pen's trumpeting of 'national preference' and in Trump's slogan 'make America great again'. Let us take the French National Front (FN) as our example.

As early as 1997, a leading spokeman for the FN explained that 'national preference is the nuclear core of our programme'.[3] This is well put: the essence of fascism is extreme nationalism – an attempt to realise the myth of the nation by authoritarian power, racial exclusion, and violent action. Everything else is contingent and changeable; in motion, as it were, around the stable core. Fascism can adopt a 'right' face or a 'left' face as appropriate, dependent on the audience, the issue, the wider context. The combination of stagnation-slump and social discontent requires a left face – more precisely, a national-socialist face, where the emphasis is on national economic development and a promise of social improvement for native workers.

This shift, under way through the 1990s and 2000s, has accelerated since the election of Marine Le Pen as FN leader in 2011. The party is increasingly anti-globalisation and pro-state; it now defends the public sector and favours increased government spending. The party's strong anti-EU stance – with Le Pen promising a 'Frexit' referendum if she wins the presidency – and its support for rapprochement with Russia are both expressions of the isolationism inherent in 'autarchy' (economic nationalism).

This does not mean that the fascists are able to advance a coherent economic programme. The relationship with globalised corporate power is complex and contradictory. In the 1930s, when most units of big capital were still firmly anchored in a single national market, a 'state-capitalist' programme of economic development was far more viable. Variants of it proved effective in overcoming the collapse in investment and employment following the 1929 Crash. Stalinist Russia avoided the depression almost entirely. Nazi Germany recovered rapidly and had eliminated unemployment by 1939. And if Roosevelt's New Deal was in relative terms a damp squib, the 'military Keynesianism' of the Second World War (and later of the Cold War) – where government arms-contracts acted as a major economic stimulus – did eventually pull the US economy out of the depression and prevent it collapsing back into another later.

No such state-capitalist fix is available today. Big capital nowadays is typically a trans-global conglomerate with major operations in a dozen countries. The state has ceased to be an economic actor in its own right and become instead a sponsor, a client, a wooer of the private corporation. So Trump threatens the stick of tariffs on the one hand, but offers the carrot of deregulation on the other. If profits are liable to take a hit from higher costs in US plants, the solution is to bring the costs down in other ways – by, for example, trashing environmental protection, eroding labour rights, and squeezing wages.

The national-socialist turn of the Far Right will be incomplete. The fascists cannot reverse globalisation. They cannot use the state to dominate capital in the way their predecessors did in the 1930s. This is one reason that cultural racism – anti-migrant and anti-Muslim – is so central to the programme of the Far Right today.

## CULTURAL RACISM

The mythic nation is defined by difference. Here is the point where everyday racism intersects with nationalist ideology. Everyday racism arises from the divisions inside the working class, the competition for jobs, homes, better conditions, and so on that are a feature of life under capitalism, and of the way in which this experience is refracted through the lens of reactionary 'commonsense' bourgeois ideology. Fascism clarifies, organises, and mobilises this everyday racism and puts it to work in the service of nationalism.

Biological racism – the pseudo-scientific notion that some races are superior to others – is too discredited, too tainted by Nazism, to be useful. Cultural racism has, in fact, been dominant since the Second World War, and it is central to far-right discourse today. The Far Right defines the nation as a community with its own history, religious affiliations, cultural traditions, and a defined set of values; a community so different from others that the immigration and attempted integration of outsiders pose a mortal threat to the survival and wellbeing of the nation.

Geert Wilders, the authoritarian leader of the Dutch Party of Freedom (PVV), has flourished by making the transition from neoliberal ultra to a politician who espouses a mixture of visceral Islamophobia, welfare chauvinism, and fascist liberalism. This oil-and-water cocktail becomes comprehensible only in relation to the Dutch nationalism which forms the core of Wilders' politics.

For Wilders, the integrity of the Dutch nation is threatened both by an existing community of Moroccans and by further Muslim immigration. All Muslims are enemies because 'their behaviour flows from their religion and culture'. As well as harbouring a terrorist threat and fostering a wave of street crime, Muslims are considered to be unassimilable because they are inherently misogynist, homophobic, anti-semitic, and authoritarian in their politics. It is this that explains the PVV's fascist 'liberalism' – the fact, for example, that it offers rhetorical support for gay rights. Tolerance and democracy are held to be distinctive characteristics of the Dutch national identity – in relation to which the Muslim 'Other' is portrayed as benighted and backward.

Welfare chauvinism – adopted in place of neoliberalism as PVV party policy in 2010 – fits this perspective: 'Dutchness' is bound up with a modern form of citizenship that includes various social benefits inherent in membership of the national community. These benefits, of course, are not to be enjoyed by those who do not belong. Wilders favours closing Islamic schools, recording the ethnicity of all citizens, making social security dependent on length of citizenship and language skills, and denying it altogether to women wearing a burka or niqab.[4] His response to Trump's Muslim travel ban was to tweet: 'Well done. It's the only way to stay safe and free. No more immigration from any Islamic country is exactly what we need. For Islam and freedom are incompatible.'[5]

This kind of cultural anti-migrant racism has contaminated the whole of mainstream politics. As early as June 1991, for instance, Jacques Chirac, a former prime minister, a future president, and at the time the mayor of Paris, spoke of the French Parisian

> who works with his wife and who, altogether, earns around 15,000 francs, and who sees on the landing along- side in his low-income housing block, piled up, a family with a father, three or four wives, and about 20 kids, and who earns 50,000 francs in state benefits, without ever working! If you add to that the noise and the smell, of course the French worker on the landing goes mad...[6]

Chirac's racism was spasmodic. Sarkozy, his successor as president, was more consistent, talking of '50 years of insufficiently regulated immigration', and introducing a law in 2010 that banned the wearing of the burka on French soil. The National Front was in no doubt of the effect:

> Sarkozy's statements on the relation between immigration and delinquency favour and give credibility to the FN... Sarkozy serves as an ice-breaker for the Front, and he is not conscious of it... That gives legitimacy to our arguments...that shows that our programme is not so bad, when the president has just adopted it... We must keep up the pressure to make the Right implode. The recomposition will take place around us, our ideas.[7]

Islamophobia is the anti-semitism of modern fascism. Steve Bannon, the Goebbels of the Trump regime, has said as much. Bannon, former executive of Breitbart, the leading fake-news website of America's 'Alt-Right' and now chief strategist and ideological guru inside the White House, has declared that 'we're now at the beginning stages of a global war against Islamic fascism'.[8] The politics here are indistinguishable from those of Hitler's 'international Jewish conspiracy'. Trump's travel ban has to be seen in this light. It is the Nuremberg Laws or the *Kristallnacht*.[9]

The effect of the US presidential executive order signed on 27 January 2017 banning the citizens of seven Muslim-majority countries from entering the United States was to stigmatise an entire religious community, an estimated 1.6 billion of the world's people, as pariahs. It was the moment, said Sudanese writer Nesrine Malik, when the tide of Islamophobia rising for a decade 'finally burst its banks'.[10] It is the logic inherent, for example, in the construction of 'Fortress Europe' and the Euro-elite's deal with the Turkish dictatorship, which is being paid to prevent Middle Eastern refugees from reaching Europe and to hold them instead in massive, insanitary, overcrowded concentration camps inside Turkey.[11]

The ban has nothing to do with security. As the *Guardian*'s Julian Borger reported,

A western official pointed out that Muslim-majority nations where Trump has business interests – such as Egypt, Saudi-Arabia, and Turkey – were excluded, while noting that no terrorist attacks on US soil have been carried out by nationals of the seven countries in the executive order.[12]

The purpose of the ban is to ratchet up racism, reduce immigration, and shift society further to the right. It has nothing to do with security, except in so far as security panics are the twin of Islamophobia in far-right discourse. So far from making us safer, the point is to feed a 'clash of civilisations' state of tension. The Islamists and the Far Right are mutually reinforcing poles. The right-wing terrorists of ISIS reap the harvest from the bitterness sown by Islamophobic racism. The Far Right scoops up further support each time a lorry is driven into a market, a bomb set off in a night-club, or machine-gun fire sprayed across a beach.

## WELFARE CHAUVINISM

The far-right surge is rooted in economic stagnation and social distress. The Resolution Foundation has calculated that real earnings in Britain will be

> no higher in 2020-21 than they were in 2006-07...that pay growth over the decade from 2010 would be the weakest since the 1900s. Total growth of just 1.6% in the decade to 2020 compares with growth of 12.7% in the 2000s and over 20% in every other decade since the 1920s.[13]

Nor is it simply that the economy is in slump; it is also that society's inequalities are widening rapidly. As another recent study revealed of the United States:

> The bottom half of the income distribution in the United States has been completely shut off from economic growth since the 1970s. From 1980 to 2014, average national income per adult grew by 61% in the United States, yet the average pre-tax income of the bottom 50% of individual income-earners stagnated at about $16,000 per adult after adjusting for inflation. In contrast, income skyrocketed at the top of the income distribution, rising 121% for the top 10%, 205% for the top 1%, and 636% for the top 0.001%.[14]

This 'bottom half' demographic is being actively courted by the Far Right. Despite its image as the Tory Party in exile, UKIP is in fact more working-class in composition than any other major party in Britain. It has the highest proportion of manual workers and its supporters are the oldest, the most male, and the least educated.[15] Little wonder that the new UKIP leader is arguing explicitly that the party should target mainly Labour seats.

Not that there is any direct and simple relationship between the level of economic and social crisis and the strength of the Far Right. Many other variables are in play. The Far Left has been at the forefront of anti-austerity movements in some parts of Europe since 2008 – notably in Greece and Spain, where there have been both mass social movements on the streets, with Athens and Madrid at times paralysed by popular mobilisations, and, in Syriza and Podemos respectively, mass electoral parties able to secure millions of votes. Bernie Sanders' campaign for the Democratic presidential nomination in the States, and the double election of Jeremy Corbyn as leader of the Labour Party in Britain, are further obvious examples of left-wing movements against austerity and inequality.

But the Left has not broken through, and across most of the continent the polarisation has favoured the Far Right. Even in Greece, a mass fascist party has become established. This is Golden Dawn, a thuggish neo-Nazi outfit that avoids the double-speak of suited fascists elsewhere in Europe and openly proclaims itself 'National-Socialist'. Golden Dawn has a paramilitary wing, its 'battalion squads', organises anti-migrant marches near refugee camps, and warns darkly of the 'Islamisation of Greece'.

Despite the unmistakable smell of interwar fascism – and Greece's history of Nazi occupation during the Second World War – Golden Dawn rocketed from 0.5% of the vote in 2009 to 9.4% in 2014. This, of course, was the period of the austerity-induced economic implosion which left one in four jobless and cut wages by a third or more – what Yanis Varoufakis, briefly the Syriza finance-minister, called 'fiscal waterboarding' on the part of European finance-capital.

Another country where direct connection between economic catastrophe and mass fascism seems obvious is Hungary. As with so many former Stalinist states, the transition from state capitalism to neoliberal capitalism belied the heady promise of liberal dissidents and reformed *apparatchiks* that the free market would be the Garden of Eden. The Hungarian economy went through the floor. More than 1.3 million jobs – almost a third of the total – disappeared during the first five years of the transition. At the same time, the social protections provided by the old regime were jettisoned in the *laissez-faire* frenzy. Hungarian society had not recovered when hit by a second sledgehammer blow, the 2008 Crash, since when poverty rates have skyrocketed, with 3.3 million Hungarians, a third of the population, now living in poverty.[16]

Stalinism imposed totalitarian dictatorships on Eastern Europe that destroyed all forms of independent working-class organisation. It also appropriated and corrupted the language of the Left, making socialism synonymous with the rule of bosses, bureaucrats, and police. When Stalinism collapsed in Eastern Europe in 1989, the task of building a real labour movement was virtually at ground zero. Consequently, when people turned on the neoliberal successor governments – corrupt crony-capitalist regimes which had enriched themselves and the oligarchs around them at the expense of everyone else – it was the Far Right that made all the headway.

Viktor Orban's Fidesz party won a landslide election victory in 2010, taking 53% of the popular vote. Orban whipped up Hungarian nationalism, granting citizenship to every ethnic Hungarian in the world, including the two million or so living in neighbouring Slovakia, Serbia, and Romania. Authoritarian, anti-EU, contemptuous of liberalism and democracy, above all vicious in its racism, especially against Muslim refugees fleeing the mayhem in the Middle East, the Orban regime created the political space for the expansion of Jobbik, its more extreme political cousin, into a mass fascist party.

Jobbik gives the fullest expression to popular disillusionment with the neoliberal political and corporate elite. It is against the free market, against liberal democracy, and against unconditional allegiance to 'the West'. It demands radical solutions and national rejuvenation. It targets intellectuals, liberals, communists, Jews, and Roma – as well as Muslim refugees – and turns these into the shock-absorbers of the accumulating anger and aggression inside Hungarian society.

Jobbik's violence is spearheaded by its 'Hungarian Guard' (renamed 'New Hungarian Guard' since it was banned). The party speaks openly of 'the Gypsy Question', arguing that 'the coexistence and cohesion of Magyar [Hungarian] and Gypsy is one of the severest problems facing Hungarian society', that 'gypsy crime' is already a major crisis, and 'virtual civil war' an imminent possibility. True to its rhetoric, Jobbik has organised a series of rallies in Roma-dominated neighbourhoods, and is behind a surge in racial attacks, including one notorious case in which nine Roma were murdered, including a five-year-old boy, and dozens of others left seriously injured.

Despite its violent racist nature, Jobbik, like Golden Dawn in Greece, has flourished, taking 21% of the popular vote in 2014, making it the third largest party. Recent polls have even placed it ahead of Orban's Fidesz. So Hungary today offers the spectacle of a ruling far-right regime where the main opposition is an even more hard-line form of fascism.

## CYBER FASCISM

Nazi-style paramilitaries are the exception today rather than the rule. They have usually arisen in circumstances of exceptional social crisis and political confrontation, and are much more prevalent in Eastern Europe, with its weaker liberal parliamentary tradition, than in the West. Even in Eastern Europe, the paramilitaries – so far at least – tend to be relatively small adjuncts of the more extreme fascist parties. There is, at present, nothing to compare with Mussolini's Blackshirts, Hitler's Brownshirts, or the Falangists of the Spanish Civil War – which numbered tens, even hundreds, of thousands.

We have discussed the reasons for this above: the more protracted, shallower nature of the crisis; the slower pace of political polarisation; the weakness of the labour movement and oppositional civil-society organisations more generally; and, not least, the toxicity of the interwar fascist brand and the concern of the more sophisticated fascist leaders to avoid its taint.

This determination to 'de-demonise' fascism – to court electoral respectability and eschew paramilitary parades, street violence, and the cruder forms of racism – is highly characteristic of modern Western fascism. In the case of the National Front, as early as 1972, when Jean Marie Le Pen founded the party by amalgamating a number of smaller fascist and paramilitary organisations, the Nazi trappings – the swastika, the iron cross, the *Sieg Heil* salutes, the white-supremacism, the hate speech, the street-fighting thugs – were dropped in favour of suits and media-savvy *bonhomie*.

The transition to 'Eurofascism' (as it was called) was incomplete. The mask sometimes slipped, and Le Pen would belch some anti-semitic obscenity, like his 1987 quip that the Holocaust was a mere 'detail in history'.[17] The party established itself as a permanent fixture, but it failed to break through, and by the late 2000s, many cadre came to believe that the ageing bigot was holding them back. Marine Le Pen's election as party president in 2011 was, in fact, a usurpation.

Since then, the younger Le Pen, guided by the sinister Florian Philippot, has driven forwards a programme of *dédiabolisation* ('de-demonisation'). Charismatic, articulate, media-friendly, Marine Le Pen now denies her party is 'fascist' or even 'extreme right' and makes a direct pitch for mainstream French opinion. She typically sounds well to the left of Donald Trump. She has certainly positioned herself as a national-socialist, appealing for support from the traditional working class, as against a neo-liberal mainstream, both conservative and socialist, that offers nothing to the 'just about managing' of the age of austerity – so much so that François Hollande likened the FN manifesto to a 'Communist tract of the 1970s'.[18]

The racist message has been recoded. Instead of the vicious abuse of the old-school fascist, Le Pen claims that she is not opposed to Islam as such, only to Islamism and Islamisation. She wants a crackdown on Muslims and reduced benefits and health care for immigrants, but this is centred on a core belief in a distinctive national culture that is under threat. 'The immigrationist religion [multiculturalism] is,' she says, 'an insult to human beings, whose integrity is always bound to one national community, one language, one culture.'

What is also clear is that modern fascism is less activist. Not only are the massed paramilitaries largely absent, but public gatherings of any kind are less central. They are not entirely lacking. The *Manif Pour Tous* demonstrations against gay marriage in 2013 (discussed elsewhere) were mass mobilisations of a far-right alliance, albeit one dominated by the Church and conservative ultras rather than the National Front, which was represented in the events mainly by Le Pen's niece, the devoutly Catholic and socially conservative Marion Maréchal-Le Pen. In the United States, the Trump election rallies, the Trump inauguration crowd on 20 January 2017, and the Pro-Life demonstration on 27 January 2017 can all be considered, in some sense, far-right mobilisations.

We should expect more of this, especially if the resistance rises and the Left becomes a serious threat. The Far Right will then be forced to try to bring their supporters onto the streets, in an effort to win moral, even physical, hegemony.

But in the business of movement-building, for the present at least, the balance seems to have shifted from marches and rallies to a more privatised form of fascism – a form that fits, perhaps, the hollow society we described in the previous chapter. We call this 'cyber fascism'.

In a speech in Reno, Nevada, on 25 August 2016, Hillary Clinton, the Democratic Party candidate in the presidential election, claimed that Trump had built his campaign on prejudice and paranoia, and that he was 'making hate groups mainstream and helping a radical fringe take over the Republican Party'. She had turned over a stone and exposed the creatures lurking beneath, now brought blinking into daylight from the dark recesses of the internet. It was a watershed moment: America's 'Radical Right' – or 'Alt-Right' (Alternative Right) – was suddenly visible in a glare of global media attention. It is now ensconced in the White House, represented by Steve Bannon, a hard-core fascist, racist, and misogynist, who has been installed as Trump's leading lieutenant and ideologue.

The Alt-Right is mainly an online phenomenon, where tech-savvy white men (occasionally women) post and discuss white-supremacist and patriarchal material on sites like YouTube, Twitter, Reddit, 4chan, 8chan, and a plethora of blogs and webzines. They have established a sub-cultural hegemony in parts of the internet by virtue of the quantity and quality of the material they churn out. And as millennials and others increasingly get their news and opinion from online sources, and increasingly interact with the world not through direct contact but through social media, the Alt-Right has a vast audience for its bigotry, its fabrications, and its conspiracy theories.

Richard Spencer is an archetype of this virtual netherworld. He was briefly in the limelight when filmed at an unofficial Trump victory event proclaiming 'Hail Trump! Hail our people! Hail our victory!' before an eager audience responding with *Sieg Heil* salutes. But he prefers the shadows. Not only is he anti-liberal; he despises mainstream conservatism for its accommodation to diversity, democracy, and free-market capitalism. Spencer considers these to be 'anti-ideals'. The job of the Alt-Right is to create a new kind of conservative. And he welcomes Trump because he has opened the space for this to happen.

Spencer and his ideological allies define themselves as 'white identitarians' – they are white-supremacists who respond to the identity politics of the oppressed by advocating identity politics for white men. They maintain that the white race is under threat from immigration. The more hysterical speak of 'white genocide'. They consider themselves to have moved beyond the crude anti-black racism of the Ku Klux Klan: their aim is to make America white again.

Breitbart, of which Steve Bannon is a former executive, and its poster-boy, Milos Yiannopoulos, represent a less extreme, more popular version of Alt-Right ideology. White-supremacism, anti-semitism, and homophobia are rejected – Yiannopoulos is, in fact, both Jewish and openly gay – but Breitbart shares the view that Western democracy and culture are threatened by immigration, Islamism, and the 'politically correct' liberal Left. Breitbart is a mass phenomenon, getting millions of hits, and acts as gateway to the harder Alt-Right.

Trump's tweets – with 15 million followers and rising – and his refusal to engage with the mainstream media except on his own terms is the most high-profile expression of the new cyber-fascism. The Far Right is communicating directly with its supporters, feeding them messages – bile, lies, fake news, carefully selected and decontextualised information – that confirm prejudices and nurture ignorance. Dr Goebbels' radio broadcasts have been replaced by Alt-Right webzines.

## THE STRONG STATE

Fascism requires a strong state. Fascism seeks to override the sectional divisions of class society by forging a united 'nation'. But the divisions are real and the nation is a myth, so an external force is required to unify society – to crush the labour movement, silence dissidents, and cow minorities. This is why fascism is inherently authoritarian and hostile to liberalism and democracy as well as to socialism and the unions.

Fascism's authoritarian reflexes were evident in the first days of the Trump regime. Journalists, lawyers, and civil servants – the personnel of liberal parliamentary democracy – were under attack from the outset. Six journalists arrested during anti-Trump protests on inauguration day were charged with felony riot offences carrying a 10-year prison sentence.[19] This is now part of an established pattern. Film-makers and live-streamers arrested while covering anti-pipeline protests last autumn are among those about to go on trial in Washington State.[20] The unmistakable message? Those who report on opposition to the regime risk incarceration.

The regime is equally contemptuous of the judiciary. There were reports from across the United States that Customs and Border Protection (CBP) officials simply ignored the orders of federal judges and continued illegally detaining people at airports in conformity with Trump's Muslim refugee and immigration ban. When Acting Attorney-General Sally Yates questioned the legality of the ban and refused to defend it in court, she was sacked by the White House.[21] The unmistakable message? That the separation of powers and the independence of the judiciary – basic tenets of liberal constitutionalism – are no longer sacrosanct.

To understand the implications – and to realise how quickly liberal parliamentary democracy could crumble – one has only to look at Turkey. Here is one of a number of regimes that form part of what has been called 'an authoritarian international' – along with Vladimir Putin's Russia. Recep Tayyip Erdogan founded the Justice and Development Party (AKP) in 2001 as a conservative Islamist party and led it to general-election victories in 2002, 2007, and 2011. Erdogan served as Turkish prime minister from 2003 to 2014, and since then has been Turkish president.

Fifteen years ago, Turkey was a functioning parliamentary democracy, but Erdogan, with the support of a passive, backward, traditionalist electorate, has become increasingly authoritarian. If not before, then certainly after the attempted coup in July 2016, the AKP regime transitioned to what is effectively a party dictatorship. The coup had been mounted by the military, but the main targets of the subsequent purge were journalists, lawyers, academics, teachers, and left activists. About 100,000 people lost their jobs, and some 40,000 were detained. Kurdish areas were put under military occupation, and the mainly Kurdish far-left People's Democratic Party (HDP) has been reduced to harried, semi-clandestine existence, with many members, including elected MPs, under arrest.

What we described in Chapter 4 as 'the hollow society' and 'the political void' appear to mean that parties of the Far Right, once they assume state power, will be capable of constructing an authoritarian state easily and rapidly. Much of the basic architecture is, it seems, already in place – in the form of the 'national security state', which has always been there, but which has greatly extended its reach in the years of the self-proclaimed 'War on Terror'.

## TRAJECTORIES

A narrow view of fascism defines it as a reactionary mass movement of the 'petty-bourgeoisie' and sections of the 'lumpenproletariat' which is semi-militarised and deployed as a battering-ram for smashing labour organisation in the interests of capital. It becomes necessary, the argument goes, when a revolutionary working-class movement arises in the context of capitalist crisis to threaten the existing social order. If this definition were correct, our concept of 'creeping fascism' would be false, since the current situation is clearly not one of para-military 'battering-ram' fascism confronting a revolutionary working class. We are convinced, however, that this definition – really a caricature of the classical theory developed by Trotsky – is misleading at every turn.

A fundamental mistake is to over-rationalise the phenomenon: to assume that fascism must somehow be *necessary* for the system; that it must be a *direct* expression of class interests. But capitalist society is not rational: it is riddled with contradiction and madness. The destruction of Syria in its five-year civil war has not been rational even in capitalist terms (unless, perhaps, you are an arms manufacturer). The Brexit vote and the threat to the free movement of goods, services, investment, and labour across the Channel is not rational from the perspective of most British capitalists. Fascism embodies such contradictions. The smashing of the unions in 1930s Germany may have been rational for German capitalism, but the extermination of the Jews in the 1940s most certainly was not. Mussolini's dictatorship may have saved the Italian ruling class from revolution, but his imperialist war led to military defeat, foreign invasion, and a communist-led national insurgency.

Fascism is not a 'tool' designed for a specific historical task. It is not 'controlled' by capitalist puppet-masters. It is a concentrated expression of what Marx called 'the shit of ages' – nationalism, racism, xenophobia, sexism, militarism, deference, power-worship – which wells up from the sewer-depths of the capitalist system in periods of crisis. This magnetic core attracts a human dust of atomised, alienated, anomic people around it, the detritus of decaying social layers at the base of the system.

If there is polarisation to the left as well as to the right, the vanguard of the proto-fascist agglomeration is likely to harden into a paramilitary 'battering-ram' directed against the labour movement. If that is not the case, if the polarisation is mainly to the right, if no great threat to the system arises on the left, the far-right movement is bound to develop in a different way. The weakness of the Left allows the Far Right to remain suited and respectable, to enter the mainstream, to become 'normalised'. This does not make it less dangerous: it simply means that events are unfolding differently.

The bubble economy, the hollow society, the political void – these, as explained in Chapter 4, are the three main building-blocks of our conceptual understanding of the present conjuncture. Of critical importance is the degree to which the neoliberal counter-revolution unleashed in the late 1970s has weakened civil society in general and the labour movement in particular.

The international ruling class broke through in the 1980s, inflicting a succession of crippling defeats on the working class, and the quarter century since has seen a massive redistribution of wealth and power in favour of capital. We suspect that we may now be witness to a second phase in that counter-revolution – a radical intensification of the atomisation, disempowerment, and de-politicisation of the working class.

The logic of neoliberal capitalism has not been changed by the 2008 Crash: it remains a globalised and financialised system of competitive capital-accumulation in the interests of the super-rich. What has changed is that the political framework of the system – parliamentary democracy, the nation-states, supra-state bodies like the EU – faces a crisis of legitimacy. Popular consent, slowly draining down over years of dreary technocratic politics under figures like Tony Blair and Bill Clinton, has been suddenly sucked away by a new, vicious, relentless austerity programme.

On one side, banks are bailed out, corporate power expands, and the rich get richer. On the other, public services are privatised, housing becomes unaffordable, prices soar, wages stagnate, and the poor get screwed. Great pools of bitterness and dissent accumulate in the social depths. The conservatives, liberals, and fake 'socialists' of the mainstream parties who preside over this travesty look like tawdry racketeers – part of a corrupt political elite in the pocket of speculators and asset-strippers.

But the system cannot run on coercion alone. Without some form of mass consent, the whole capitalist order is destabilised. Most people, most of the time, must be persuaded that their interests are served by the existing system, lest they mobilise against it. That, after all, is the whole purpose of all that 'shit of ages' – the whole panoply of myths and prejudices by which people are persuaded that the way things are is the way they should be.

When things as they are come to seem intolerable, the old must be rebranded as the new. When consent is withdrawn from 'the old gang', a cohort of 'new men' must be summoned. Capital is adaptable. It can thrive under many different political systems – under parliamentary democracies, under military dictators, under fascist rule. Whatever the regime, what matters is that the mix of coercion and consent – of 'force and fraud' – is sufficient to stabilise society, manage dissent, and suppress resistance. The rule of capital is absolute: the form of politics is relative.

Creeping fascism arises when society is hollowed-out and the political system has become a void. It arises not because there is resistance – from a militant working-class movement – but precisely because there is none. The Far Right grows to fill the political space created by the collapse of a discredited Centre. It offers a new form of consent – a repackaging of 'the shit of ages', but also a supercharging of it, such that the anger at the base is channelled not against the system, but against its victims.

Paramilitary thugs have always been secondary components of fascist repression. The state apparatus has always been the primary instrument for the suppression of liberal democracy and labour organisation. This was true in every case of interwar fascism – in Italy in 1922, in Germany in 1933, in Spain in 1936. It remains true today. The real danger now is not a strengthening of fascist paramilitaries. It is far-right control of the state police. The real worry is that the police unions backed Trump and they control stockpiles of surplus military equipment.

We have argued that fascism is a process; that it varies according to circumstances, that it changes over time, that it is a flexible political movement that evolves in interaction with other forces. We see a contrast between the interwar situation, where far-right movements were engaged in a direct struggle with revolutionary forces *before they came to power*, and the very different situation today, where far-right movements are advancing *directly on state power*. As they do this, they pull the entire mainstream political system to the right, increasing the level of racism, stirring the human dust of the social crisis into a whirlwind of hate.

This – especially in the context of the bubble economy, the hollow society, and the political void – is building a reactionary momentum. Unable to break with neoliberal capital, the Far Right will not be able to solve the economic and social crisis. What they will be able to do is to appease the passions of the mass movement they are creating. To create jobs, build affordable homes, or reduce poverty will be far harder than to unleash the security state on migrants and Muslims.

We face a tidal wave of racism and reaction. This wave has been generated by the socio-political turbulence of a world capitalist crisis. Far-right control of the state can only increase the energy of the wave.

There are no hard lines of separation between fascism, far-right populism, and traditional conservatism: they are points on a spectrum. Historically, far-right movements have proved diverse and changeable. The current direction of travel is obvious – towards the right, towards more nationalism, racism, sexism, xenophobia, authoritarianism, and securitisation. The chain of influence is pulling all the time to the right. The do-nothing Centre is capitulating to the racism, and thereby amplifying the far-right message that the problem is the beggars not the bankers. There is nothing to prevent the Far Right becoming harder, more radical, more murderous, as it assumes the levers of state power.

Interwar 'battering-ram' fascism – that of the Italian Fascists, the German Nazis, and the Spanish Falangists – was an explosion directed at a revolutionary working-class movement. The 'creeping' fascism of the present is the implosion of a society already hollowed out. Be in no doubt: in the void, a monster is rising.

# CHAPTER 6
# Is it really fascism?

In this chapter, we address head-on the question whether or not contemporary movements of the Far Right can be described as 'fascist'. Politics is both an art and a science. Action (or practice) must be based on analysis (theory). It is necessary to characterise political tendencies accurately if we are to develop effective strategies for opposing them.

'Fascist' is widely used as a term of abuse. The government is 'fascist'. The police are 'fascist'. The state is 'fascist'. But usually they are not. And the danger in using the term in this way is that it loses meaning – becoming a description of any right-wing phenomenon we do not like – and this leads to muddled thinking in the face of the real thing.

We want to stress the point about theoretical clarity. In Chapter 7, drawing on historical experience, we will discuss strategy and tactics for defeating fascism. We will describe a distinct repertoire of methods appropriate to dealing with this particular form of right-wing politics – a repertoire that it would be inappropriate to apply in a struggle against mainstream right-wing forces. To use a military metaphor, we need an accurate assessment of the character and capacity of the enemy before launching a counterattack.

On the other hand, as argued in earlier chapters, we must reject any simplistic definition of fascism that depends upon externals like badges, uniforms, and parades. Those who imagine that the enemies of the working class will announce themselves like pantomime baddies, painted green and dressed in black, when they walk onto history's stage are dangerous fools. Fascism, to repeat, is a process, a motion, a trajectory, not a finished form. It evolves in relation to the crisis, to the opportunities it throws up, to interactions with other forces, to collisions with those who stand in its way. Appearances and forms are very varied. Fascism is defined by its essence: by the fact that it is an authoritarian-reactionary mass movement formed of the human dust stirred into motion by the capitalist crisis and organised around the myths of nation and race.

It is not enough simply to compare contemporary movements with an image of interwar fascism – an image which tends, in any case, to be caricature. Especially so as there are at least three major differences between the 1930s and the 2010s which bear heavily on the form of modern fascism.

The first is memory. Every schoolchild knows what happened in the Nazi death-camps. Every adult has seen the grainy black-and-white footage of industrialised mass murder. Each generation, when the lesson is taught, experiences the horrified reaction of BBC radio audiences listening to Richard Dimbleby's report from Bergen-Belsen in April 1945.[1] We live in the shadow of the Holocaust. Though there is a neo-Nazi fringe, the brand is toxic, poisoned by history's greatest atrocity, and open advocacy of fascist ideology is usually political suicide. Serious fascists know this.

This is why most Italian fascists, previously organised in the MSI (*Movimento Sociale Italiano*), which used to celebrate its direct descent from Mussolini's Fascists, followed Gianfranco Fini into the 'post-fascist' National Alliance (*Alleanza Nazionale*). It is why Marine Le Pen, since becoming leader of France's National Front in 2011, has sought to detoxify a party tainted by anti-semitism, violence, and corruption, relaunching it as a respectable 'national preference' party appealing for support to mainstream voters on both the right and the left. It is why Nigel Farage cultivates the image of a cheery chappy who likes a fag and a pint, and avoids association with any organisation, at home or abroad, which bears the mark of the swastika, even including 'cleaned-up' formations like Fini's National Alliance and Le Pen's National Front.

The Nazi Holocaust is perhaps the world's most visceral historical memory. Modern fascism must negotiate its way around this. That is one critical difference between the present and the interwar period. Another is the nature of the world capitalist crisis today.

After the 1929 Crash, the two biggest economies in the world went over a cliff. In both Germany and the United States, unemployment exceeded one in four of the workforce by 1932. In Germany, the crisis, compounded by debt and austerity, tore society apart and paralysed the parliamentary system. This led to rapid political polarisation and high levels of popular mobilisation. In the May 1928 general election, the Communists had taken less than 11% of the vote, the Nazis less than 3%, making them the fourth and ninth largest parties respectively. The Social Democrats were first, the conservative DNVP second, the Catholic Centre Party third, and the conservative DVP fifth. By the time of the July 1932 election, the German political system had been turned upside down. The Communists now secured third position with in excess of 14% of the vote, while the Nazis soared into first place with more than 37%. The Social Democratic and Centre Parties largely held their ground, but the traditional conservative parties went into meltdown.

The electoral polarisation was reflected in the savagery of the struggle on the streets. The climax came when Nazi Brownshirts attempted to march through the solidly working-class suburb of Altona in Hamburg on 17 July 1932. A Communist activist described what happened:

> Units of Red Front Fighters [the Communist Party paramilitaries] were stationed in advance on the roofs of the houses along the route of the Storm-troop invasion... The

Storm-troops marched...with bands crashing and swastikas flying. Their demonstration was flanked by police. Police lorries with machine-guns preceded and followed the marchers.

The parade entered the sinuous old districts of the city, winding forward like an immense brown snake... The side streets along the route seethed with many thousands of workers and their womenfolk shaking fists, hurling rocks and garbage at the Brownshirts, and shouting their abuse.

The Storm-troops marched like one machine. The faces of the youngsters were set and pale. At minute intervals, at a signal of detachment leaders, they broke into a hollow roar: 'Death to the Red Pest! Germany – arise!'

Then the first shots cracked from the roofs. The Storm-troopers crowded into houses to trap the attackers on the roofs. Garbage cans were hurled out of the windows, policemen hurled gas grenades, and people ran like cockroaches. The Storm-troopers were broken up in irregular, badly shaken groups. Some continued their march. Most of them fled...[2]

At the end of the day's fighting, 19 people were dead, 15 of them Nazis. The picture in Germany in 1932 is of sudden economic collapse, acute social distress, and violent political confrontation.

The crisis this time is playing out differently. It is slower and shallower. The international political elite responded to the 2008 Crash by deploying vast quantities of public money to prop up a bankrupt financial system. The vast overhang of bad debt revealed by the crash was transformed – virtually overnight – from an obligation on billionaire speculators to an obligation on working-class taxpayers. To prevent the ruin of the few, austerity was imposed on the many.

The economic effect was to achieve a degree of fragile

stability in an inherently dysfunctional, parasitic, and stagnant system of debt-based casino capitalism. No underlying problems were addressed. No real, long-term solutions were offered. So, though the system avoided wholesale collapse after 2008, the result was merely to make the crisis more protracted.

Financialisation is consuming the sinews of society like dry rot consumes the woodwork of an ancient building. The thing can be propped up, perhaps indefinitely, but it cannot be made good. And the decay takes the form of a spreading, festering mass of discontent at the base of the social order, and a consequent leaching away of support for its political structures.

The crisis of capitalism in the 1930s was first and foremost an abrupt economic collapse. The crisis of capitalism in the 2010s is first and foremost a deepening social malaise. This difference of conjuncture means that fascism is bound to take on different forms.

A third difference between the 1930s and the present is this: when the economy crashed in 1929, the international labour movement created in the great wave of struggle between 1917 and 1923 had not yet suffered decisive defeat. For sure, there had been a series of individual defeats – in Italy in 1922, in Germany in 1923, in Britain in 1926, in China in 1927. And for sure, the Russian Revolution had been defeated, the mass working-class movement of 1917 drowned in blood, a monstrous totalitarian dictatorship erected on the wreckage. But the balance of power in the global class struggle had not yet tipped irretrievably against the Left.

In Germany, 13 million workers voted for the parties of the Left in the July 1932 general election. An estimated 130,000 were enrolled in the Communist Party militia, the Red Front Fighters, alone. That the German labour movement capitulated to the Nazi coup without a fight six months later was due not to inherent weakness but because it was crippled by its leadership – by the congenital spinelessness of the Social Democrats, and by the sectarian stupidity of the Communists.

The workers elsewhere learnt the lesson of the German catastrophe. In Austria, in February 1934, tens of thousands of armed workers battled the army, the police, and fascist para-militaries in an attempt to stop a right-wing coup. They failed, but at least they fought. 'Better Vienna than Berlin!' became an anti-fascist rallying cry of the European Left.

That same month, in Paris, an attempted fascist coup trig-gered a general strike and two huge demonstrations, called by the Socialist and Communist Parties respectively. The demon-strations merged spontaneously into one amid an explosion of shouts and applause and cries of 'Unity! Unity!' Two years later, in May-June 1936, following victory for the parties of the Left in a general election, two million French workers joined a general strike, and three-quarters of the strike-bound factories were occupied. The British ambassador compared the situation to that in Russia in 1917.

A month later, in Spain, hundreds of thousands of workers, peasants, and rural labourers rose in revolt against an attempted military takeover. *No pasaran!* – 'They shall not pass!' – became the slogan of the anti-fascist militias defending Madrid. And when, in October 1936, at the Battle of Cable Street, the work-ers of East London fought the police to a standstill to prevent Mosley's Blackshirts from marching, they too chanted 'They shall not pass!'

The Spanish Left was defeated in early 1939 and a fascist-backed military dictatorship established under General Franco. The French succumbed to German invasion in May-June 1940, and the country was partitioned between a Nazi administration in the north and the collaborationist Vichy regime of Marshal Pétain in the south. But the fascists were defeated on the streets of Britain in 1936, and the Nazi bomber offensive was defeated by the people of London in 1940, leaving Britain a military plat-form from which an invasion of Nazi-occupied Europe could eventually be mounted.

The situation today is the reverse. In place of a militant

mass movement of the working class, we have unions weakened by 35 years of defeat and retreat, socialist parties hollowed out by neoliberalism, and the post-war promise of economic betterment and social justice shattered by casino capitalism and corporate greed. The decisive class battles that shaped our era were fought in the 1980s, above all in Britain, where a succession of powerful trade unions were drawn into action and smashed – the steelworkers, the miners, the printers, the dockers, and others – reconfiguring the balance of forces so to enable a full-scale offensive to be mounted against the welfare state.

We looked at the long-term consequences of these events in Chapter 4, where we attempted to describe the neoliberal dystopia in terms of the bubble economy, the hollow society, and the political void. The significance of that analysis is now clear. In early 1930s Germany, the paramilitaries of the Left, the Iron Front of the Social Democrats and the Red Front Fighters of the Communists, may have numbered 300,000 or more. That is why Hitler needed 400,000 Brownshirts. Italy in 1922, Germany in 1933, and Spain in 1936 required 'battering-ram' fascism because it was confronted by a mass, militant, mobilised Left. Nothing remotely like this level of social and political polarisation exists today. Fascism is growing inside a hollow society and advancing to power in a political void; it is seeping through the pores of a rotten body-politic; it is creeping its way to political hegemony with minimal resistance.

But this means it is not fascism, some argue. Precisely because the crisis is less acute, the workers less of a threat, our rulers have no need of a fascist battering-ram. And it this characteristic, the battering-ram, that defines fascism. Without this, you may have far-right populism, you may have working-class racism, but you do not have fascism.

We must examine this argument in detail. If it is correct, we may relax our guard. If it is wrong – and we are convinced that it is wrong – we are liable to suffer the fate that Trotsky predicted when he warned the German Communist Party in 1931 that 'if fascism comes to power, it will ride over your skulls and spines like a terrific tank'.[3] We shall break the argument down into three component elements.

## IS THE LEFT A THREAT TO THE SYSTEM IN THE EARLY 21ST CENTURY?

Classical interwar fascism developed in the context of a global revolutionary challenge. The carnage of the First World War, the misery of the post-war depression, and the example of the Russian Revolution inspired a great wave of working-class struggle for radical change. Mass movements of the Left promised a radical transformation. Mussolini, Hitler, and Franco represented the counter-revolutionary response of the Right. Their essential historical role was to destroy the labour movements in Italy, Germany, and Spain. Surely the situation today is radically different – far from that polarisation between the party of revolutionary hope (the socialists) and the party of counter-revolutionary despair (the fascists) described by Trotksy in the 1930s?

What is clear is that the unions are much weaker and the socialist parties much more discredited than in the interwar period. But this does not prevent an accumulation of discontent at the base of society. The crisis leaves people feeling alienated, embittered, and angry. Many seek ways to fight back. When the opportunity is offered, hundreds of thousands are willing to protest.

The neoliberal era, especially since 1999, has been an age of protest like no other. The system has been buffeted by three great waves of mass action from below. The first began with the 40,000-strong Seattle 'teamsters and turtles' demonstration against the World Trade Organisation in November 1999. Police violence turned the event into a major street battle, watched on screens across the world, which launched a new 'anti-globalisation' or 'anti-capitalist' movement. This peaked in July 2001 with a 200,000-strong protest in Genoa against the

G8 Summit – notable for the murder by riot police of 23-year-old activist Carlo Giuliani.

The movement faltered in the wake of the 9/11 terrorist attack on the Twin Towers in New York. But when this was used to justify a Western military attack on first Afghanistan (in October 2001) and then Iraq (in March 2003), the militancy that had flowed into the anti-capitalist movement found a new channel – the struggle against imperialism and war. On 15 February 2003, during the countdown to the Anglo-American attack on Iraq, the largest co-ordinated protests in human history took place, with anywhere between 10 and 30 million people in some 600 cities on the streets. The protests included an estimated three million in Rome and between one and two million in both London and Madrid.

Over the next decade, as violence raged across a great swathe of the planet from Central Asia through the Middle East to West Africa, demonstrations of hundreds of thousands – against war, imperialism, and Zionism – would hit the streets again and again. These protests dwarfed those of the late 60s. The largest anti-Vietnam war demonstrations in Britain (in 1968) had numbered 100,000. These were considered huge at the time. The largest demonstration against the Iraq War was at least ten times this size. A national anti-war demonstration of only 100,000 in London would have been considered small in the mid 2000s.

A third wave of protest surged up in 2010. Bailouts for the rich and austerity for the rest following the 2008 Crash brought popular anger to a new level. Governments across the world, but especially in Europe, were rocked by the scale and militancy of the protests they faced. British students, furious at a tripling of university fees, smashed up the Tory Party offices during one demonstration in November 2010 and then fought a pitched battle with the police in Parliament Square a month later.

Around the same time, mass protests shook Tunis and spread rapidly from there to much of the rest of the Middle East in the 'Arab Spring' revolutions of 2010/11. The movement peaked in 18 days of revolutionary action centred on Tahrir Square in Cairo in January/February 2011, which brought the 30-year-old Mubarak dictatorship crashing down.

Where the students, youth, and workers of Egypt led, others followed, not just in the Middle East, but across the world. In autumn 2011, the Occupy Movement spread like a radical wildfire, with occupations of public squares and parks to protest against corporate power in almost a thousand cities in more than 80 countries. Between 2010 and 2013, a host of major global cities was shaken by full-scale urban insurrection. From Athens to Madrid to Istanbul to Rio, here and in a dozen other places, hundreds of thousands fought running battles with the police lasting days, sometimes weeks, turning many of the downtown heartlands of world capitalism into battlefields, the streets strewn with rocks, choked with tear gas, and echoing with the sound of sirens.

What is represented here is a sharp shift in the form of protest. The unions may be in decline and the strike rate may have plummeted, but there has been a huge increase in the numbers involved in street demonstrations and street fighting. Surveys indicate that the proportion of people taking part in street protests across the world doubled between the 1970s and the 2000s. In Britain, the proportion rose from around 2% in the early 80s to around 10% in the mid 2000s.[4] Workers may be under the cosh in the workplaces, but the urban crowd has swelled into a militant mass movement of the streets.

We live in an age of protest. The anti-capitalist, anti-war, and anti-austerity protests of the last 15 years show that the capitalism system is still – as Marx described it in *The Communist Manifesto* of 1848 – haunted by the spectre of working-class revolution.

In that sense, the politics of fascism – its poisonous cocktail of nationalism, racism, sexism, and authoritarianism – remain as relevant as ever. This is not to imply that fascism is somehow controlled by the political and corporate elite; that they manipulate it, like puppet-masters, deliberately to derail popular movements. The implication of a sinister organisation, with Machiavellian consciousness, pulling the levers of political influence behind the scenes, in the manner of a *Dr Who* story, is false. No such mechanism exists.

The argument is this. The social crisis leads to political polarisation. When this happens, the whole force of official society is on the side of the Right, partly because it is geared for the defence of property and power against threats from below, partly because fascism merely articulates in an extreme form – taking it, as it were, to its logical conclusion – the conservative ideology of the system as a whole.

## DOES THE ABSENCE OF A MASS MOVEMENT ON THE STREETS MEAN THAT TODAY'S FAR RIGHT IS NOT FASCIST?

We have argued above that paramilitary organisation is a secondary, not a defining characteristic of fascism. Fascist movements develop a paramilitary arm when they need to – to defend their meetings and marches, to attack their enemies, to galvanise their supporters, to foster tension, to create a sense of crisis – and taking due account of the drawbacks in terms of image and wider electoral appeal. A particular concern for them today is the way in which paramilitary parades and street violence tend to echo the Nazi past. Far-right leaders like Trump, Le Pen, Wilders, and Farage are desperate to avoid the toxic taint of interwar fascism.

The problem, though amplified today by historical memory, is not altogether new. The short, torrid history of the British Union of Fascists (BUF) is instructive.

Oswald Mosley was a minister in the 1929 Labour Government with special responsibility for unemployment. When his radical Keynesian programme was rejected by his pro-austerity colleagues, he resigned from both the government and the party and announced, in March 1931, that he was forming the 'New Party'.

At first, the New Party attracted the support of left-wingers like Nye Bevan and John Strachey. This soon changed. In April 1931, standing in a by-election at Ashton-under-Lyne, though the New Party bombed at the polls, its intervention split the anti-Tory vote and ensured the defeat of the Labour candidate. At the count, Mosley found himself face to face with a hostile crowd of working-class Labour supporters. 'That is the crowd that has prevented anyone doing anything in England since the war,' he told one of his followers.

The New Party then set up a defence force – the 'Biff Boys' – to protect its meetings. 'The only methods we shall employ will be English methods,' Mosley announced. 'We shall rely on the good old English fists.'

At this point, Mosley established contact with both the Italian Fascists and the German Nazis, and also began to attract some big-business support, first from Sir William Morris, the motor manufacturer, later from Lord Rothermere, the press baron. His left-wing supporters peeled away.

In October 1933, the New Party was transformed into the British Union of Fascists, complete with full trappings of black uniforms, fascist symbols, and 'Hail Mosley' salutes. This hardening into a paramilitary form of fascism was a response to Mosley's sense of the seriousness of the crisis, his inability to break the political deadlock, and the attacks of left-wing activists. As he explained as early as mid 1931:

> The Communist Party will develop a challenge in this country which will seriously alarm people here.
>
> You will in effect have the situation which arose in Italy and other countries, and which summoned into existence the modern movement which now rules in those countries.
>
> We have to build and create the skeleton of an

organisation so as to meet it when the time comes.

You have got to have an iron core in your organisation around which every element for the preservation of England will rally when a crisis of that kind comes, but that is a matter for considerable delicacy and skill.[5]

The sense of confrontation escalated in 1934, with large-scale disruption of Mosley rallies and brutal violence by his stewards. The struggle between the BUF and the Communist Party (CP) had its own logic. The BUF attracted violent men, many of them deeply racist, like the vicious anti-semite William Joyce. The CP was exceptionally strong in London's East End, home to a large working class Jewish community, so the political clashes were easily racialised in fascist rhetoric.[6]

Matters reached a climax at the Battle of Cable Street in October 1936. We discuss this in some detail in the next chapter. The salient point here is that the BUF's 'paramilitarisation' was an evolutionary development contingent upon the decisions of its leader and the challenges of the moment.

We have no doubt that all of today's Far Right movements have the capacity to develop in different ways, including towards more violent forms of fascism, according to circumstances. That they are, without exception, activist *movements* – not simply electoralist *parties* – seems to imply this.

The distinction we make here is that between political tendencies that arouse passions and expectations liable to spill onto the streets, and those which engender relative indifference and almost total passivity. Let us cite a recent example to make this point more concrete.

The Hollande government in France has been notable for its pro-austerity, anti-reform, right-wing programme. A rare exception was the bill to legalise gay marriage. In this case, on one issue at least, the aim was to push forwards not roll backwards. The effect was to bring the Far Right onto the streets in vast numbers in a campaign initiated in 2012 whose agenda quickly widened into opposition to adoption by same-sex couples, against IVF treatment, in defence of the family, and against liberal sex-education.

The *Manif Pour Tous* events – as they were known – lasted for eight months, involved three national demonstrations of 400,000 people, and gave rise to thousands of local meetings and protests. There were numerous clashes with opponents and police, and hundreds of arrests.

Though the right-wing parties, including the National Front, were divided in their response, hundreds of thousands of supporters of these parties must have responded to the call of various Catholic fundamentalist organisations – including, of course, anti-abortion campaigns – to go onto the streets. One journal, celebrating this 'Catholic Renaissance', was unequivocal about its deeply reactionary nature: 'We should understand that a new stage of the veritable war waged for two centuries against France and its Christian vocation is unfolding under our eyes.' The press described the *Manif Pour Tous* as a right-wing May 68.[7]

Like so many recent movements of the Left, the *Manif Pour Tous* went up like a rocket and down like a stick. It did not leave behind a new mass organisation. But the implications are clear. The global swing to the right is creating the potential for a more engaged, activist, street-based politics that aims to intimidate opponents, pressurise government, and harden the cadre and supporters of the Far Right.

This will be quite sufficient to maintain the momentum of the political shift and to embolden the intrinsically reactionary impulses of traditional elites and the state apparatus. Fascist paramilitaries may turn out to have no role at all. And, as it happens, the historical experience implies that more often than not they are unnecessary.

Counter-revolution takes many forms. Only occasionally have fascist paramilitaries played a significant role. The Paris Commune of 1871 was crushed by the French Army acting under government orders; an estimated 25,000 people were killed. The Shanghai Revolution of 1927 was smashed by the Chinese Nationalist troops of Chiang Kai-Chek; around 50,000 were butchered. The Popular Unity Government in Chile was overthrown in 1973 by a CIA-backed military coup; tens of thousands were arrested, many of whom were eventually murdered. There are many other examples.

Even where fascist paramilitaries do play a role – in Italy after the First World War, in Germany in the crisis of 1929-33, in Spain during the Civil War – it is always *secondary* to that of the state apparatus. Not only are there no historical examples of a fascist movement battering its way to power against the existing state; neither are there examples of fascist paramilitaries playing the predominant role in the destruction of the labour movement. What is decisive – without exception – is the *capture* of the state by the fascist movement. It was Hitler's appropriation of the official infrastructure of the army and the police that enabled him to destroy the unions, ban opposition parties, and incarcerate (and later murder) left-wing activists.

The role of the mass movement is never primarily military: it is a matter of winning consent among millions of people for the implementation of a far-right programme of extreme nationalism, racism, sexism, and authoritarianism. As one recent analysis by French Marxists explained:

> It organises in the street, in the popular neighbourhoods, sometimes in the workplace. It contests the workers' movement for public space and political space in the enterprises. Far from confining itself to the institutional, parliamentary, and media spheres, as do the classic bourgeois or reactionary parties, it seeks to mobilise society 'from below'...
>
> Once in power, fascism will moreover often maintain similar forms of organisation, but they change their function: it is no longer simply about mobilising the masses to

channel these same energies 'against the system', but of being the eyes, ears, and hands of the new regime, which tries to root itself in every neighbourhood, family, and unit of production, sometimes to detect opposition and if need be repress it, and sometimes to mobilise around the objectives of the new regime. That regime must, at regular intervals, show its ability to again mobilise the masses and appear in tune with them.[8]

We need to be aware that shifts in mass consciousness – in ways of seeing and imagining the social order – can have long-lasting effects. The work of building the great labour movements of the late 19th and early to mid 20th centuries was a work of many decades. Not before 1945 did a majority of British workers vote Labour. Not until as late as 1979 did British trade-union membership hit its all-time high. If we allow time for an alternative paradigm based on nation and race to root itself among the masses – if we allow the ideas of Farage, Trump, and Le Pen to become 'normalised' and 'mainstream' – the danger is that the ground is then laid for a sharp radicalisation of the far-right project as the crisis of the world capitalist order intensifies in the years ahead.

A final point is this. The modern state may well prove even less resistant to fascist penetration and appropriation than interwar states. The nation-state is not what it was. Globalisation and financialisation have neutered its economic role and degraded its social purpose. Big capital has de-anchored, its production facilities relocated to the low-wage 'Global East', its property-holdings scattered across the world, its cash piles stashed in offshore tax-havens. The state's core functions – police repression at home, military action overseas – remain, but capital is probably more indifferent to the political complexion of any particular government than ever before. Social-democratic, liberal, conservative, fascist: from the perspective of the global corporate elite, it hardly matters. The political void is there to be filled. As the *Guardian*'s Gary Younge put it, commenting on Trump's inauguration, 'The hands that once grabbed pussy now have access to the codes.'[9] Who needs the Klan?

## IS IT MORE ACCURATE TO SAY THAT TODAY'S FAR RIGHT CONTAINS 'THE GERM OF FASCISM' BUT IS NOT YET ACTUALLY FASCIST?

This last argument can be dealt with briefly, for we have covered much of the ground above. The idea that modern far-right parties are not yet actually fascist but might become so entails a basic conceptual mistake: to think that fascism is a fixed form rather than a political process.

Let us summarise what we have argued above. Fascism is a mass movement of the Right that arises in conditions of economic and social crisis. It constructs a movement around reactionary myths of nation, race, family, a traditional order, and an imaginary past. It seeks to fragment, disrupt, and destroy the resistance of organised labour and the Left. It is an attempt to resolve the economic and social crisis of capitalist society through the authoritarian imposition of a right-wing programme – from above, using the existing state-apparatus, but also from below, in so far as mass support legitimises and facilitates this process.

Its particular form reflects the conjuncture (the whole current situation) and the class struggle (the degree to which the fascists face resistance from the labour movement and the left parties). Fascism, in short, is not a thing, but a process; not a political movement with fixed form, but a far-right response to the crisis that develops in specific ways according to its dialectical relationship with other social forces.

The relative absence of the abrupt, stark forms of interwar fascism – Mussolini's Blackshirts, Hitler's SA, Franco's death squads – has lulled much of the Left into a false sense of security. The most extreme forms of interwar fascism are used to construct a checklist of fascist characteristics against which modern far-right movements are then compared. Is it a mass movement of an enraged middle class of farmers and small businessmen facing ruin? Does it have a uniformed paramilitary wing? Does it organise provocative marches and engage in street violence? If the answers are no, then what we face is not fascism but some sort of right-wing populism pandering to working-class racism.

This will not do. It is a static concept based on a historical caricature. As we have argued at length above, the forms of interwar fascism varied widely from place to place and over time. The same is true today. No hard-and-fast distinction can be made between traditional conservatism, right-wing populism, and fully-fledged fascism: these constitute a spectrum of overlapping tendencies organised around the myths of nationalism. In certain historical circumstances, the Right may harden into a fascist battering-ram. But in many cases, it takes the form of what we call 'creeping fascism'.

What we have in mind is a chain of influence that pulls the whole of politics to the right. On one end of the chain are the most radical sections of the Far Right – the most nationalist, racist, sexist, and authoritarian. They impact on more traditional right-wing parties and also on traditional liberal and social-democratic parties. Today, for example, by this mechanism, anti-migrant and anti-Muslim racism have been mainstreamed. All parties now advocate strong borders, controls on immigration, more resources for the police. The effect is to reinforce the dominant right-wing discourse. The central argument – that the problem is migrants not bankers, Muslims not Tories, scroungers not tax-dodgers – is confirmed. The clamour for yet more reactionary measures intensifies.

We are on a road. The direction of travel is clear. We cannot be certain of our destination or time of arrival, but we know that we are heading to the right, not the left – and history warns us what may lie at the end of the road.

## CONCLUSIONS

In a recent article in the *Los Angeles Review of Books*, Ajay Singh Chaudhary and Raphaële Chappe argue that neoliberalism has brought us half-way to fascism without any help from Trump. Their underlying observation is similar to ours: that society and the state have been hollowed out by the globalisation of capital, the atomisation of the workforce, and what we have called the 'de-politicisation' of politics. Civil society and parliamentary democracy decay because neoliberalism maintains

> ...its citizens and workforce in a state of insecurity and anxiety. Either it has better use for your time (maximum productivity) or no use for you at all (except as an economically helpful surplus population, perhaps best controlled through racialised mass incarceration).

It is not simply that the ground has been laid for fascism – but that neoliberalism has, as they put it, laid out the red carpet.

> ...we have been living in a form of deeply destructive authoritarian liberalism for nearly four decades now.
>
> ...the neoliberal state has already created a penal system to rival the world's most authoritarian dictatorships. The United States imprisons more citizens (total and per capita) than any other country on Earth, and African-Americans and Latinos at a vastly over-represented rate. Many fear Trump would bring massive deportations of undocumented immigrants. And yet, the neoliberal state already engages in mass deportations, at the level of millions during the [Obama] administration, with countless more waiting in dire conditions in the world's largest network of immigrant detention-camps. Many fear a Trump election would bring mass persecution, surveillance, and

restrictions for American Muslims. And yet, the neo-liberal state already spies on Muslims, administers religious tests at borders, and polices Muslims for nothing more than their religious practices.[10]

The Chaudhary/Chappe perspective overlaps with that developed by Sheldon Wolin, who writes of 'inverted totalitarianism' and 'quasi fascism' as the outcome of neoliberalism's hollowing out of the social order. Chauncey DeVega offered this recent summary of Wolin's theory:

> The elements are in place [for a quasi-fascist takeover]: a weak legislative body, a legal system that is both compliant and repressive, a party system in which one party, whether in opposition or in the majority, is bent upon reconstituting the existing system so as to permanently favour a ruling class of the wealthy, the well-connected, and the corporate, while leaving the poorer citizens with a sense of helplessness and political despair, and, at the same time, keeping the middle classes dangling between fear of unemployment and expectations of fantastic rewards once the new economy recovers.
>
> That scheme is abetted by a sycophantic and increasingly concentrated media; by the integration of universities with their corporate benefactors; by a propaganda machine institutionalised in well-funded think tanks and conservative foundations; by the increasingly closer co-operation between local police and national law enforcement agencies aimed at identifying terrorists, suspicious aliens, and domestic dissidents.[11]

We are in broad agreement with these perspectives. Trump represents a qualitative shift towards far more militant expressions of nationalism, racism, sexism, authoritarianism, and militarism; towards, that is, an explicitly fascist form of politics.

But that shift is a change of gear in a journey begun long ago.

The Italian Marxist theoretician Antonio Gramsci used a military metaphor to distinguish between two forms of class struggle: 'the war of manoeuvre' and 'the war of position'.

The former is the open clash of opposing classes in a decisive battle – one liable to lead to a qualitative shift in the balance of forces. The Thatcher government's attack on the miners, and on the British trade-union movement more generally, in the 1980s is an example. The latter, the war of position, is a slow, long-term process of growing influence and power by one class at the expense of the other.

The post-war period, with its strong unions, social reforms, redistributive taxation, and welfare services, represented a steady advance by the working class towards a more equal society. The neoliberal era represents the reverse: defeated in the war of manoeuvre in the 1980s, the working class has lost virtually all the ground won after the Second World War to the corporate super-rich. Another way of putting this is to say that the neoliberal counter-*revolution* of the 1980s opened the road to a sustained neoliberal counter-*evolution* over the succeeding two decades.

Our argument is that we have now arrived at a new tipping point, a qualitative shift, a fast speeding-up of the historical process, a moment when the war of position becomes again the war of manoeuvre – a moment when one class mounts an all-out offensive to win decisive victories and make rapid capture of a swathe of new territory. This, it seems to us, is the underlying implication of the far-right surge.

Those awaiting the Blackshirts before proclaiming the advent of fascism are liable to find themselves in the camps long before they raise the alarm. Trump has taken control of the most powerful state-apparatus in the world. He has no need of the Klan: he has the US police, border, and prison services at his disposal. He has already made it clear that he intends to use them.

He has, for example, denounced the Black Lives Matter movement for provoking violence against police. He has called for the reintroduction of 'stop and frisk' police searches which typically target African-Americans and Latinos. He has spoken darkly of the 'crime and gangs and drugs' that amount to 'American carnage'. He wants to 'empower our law enforcement officers to do their jobs and keep our streets free of crime and violence'. As the new White House website declared:

> The Trump Administration will be a law and order administration. President Trump will honor our men and women in uniform and will support their mission of protecting the public. The dangerous anti-police atmosphere in America is wrong. The Trump Administration will end it... Our job is not to make life more comfortable for the rioter, the looter, or the violent disrupter.[12]

Thatcher and Reagan launched the first phase of the neoliberal counter-revolution 35 years ago. Their achievement was to crush the labour movement and roll back the gains of what the French call the *Trente Glorieuses*, the 30-year period of prosperity and social reform after the Second World War. Trump is launching the second phase. He is advancing over the broken back of organised labour. He has no need of the hooded thugs of the fringe: he already controls the levers of state repression.

Whether we choose to label Trump himself a 'fascist' is neither here nor there. The man is so swollen with narcissism, so puffed up with self-importance, so obsessively preoccupied with his own ego, that to attribute any political ideology to him, even one as shallow and incoherent as fascism, seems almost perverse. But it does not matter. Trump is merely the personification of a deep-rooted historical trend – the trend that we call 'creeping fascism'.

Either the common people – the workers, the women, the

minorities, the youth – recognise the danger and organise themselves to fight, or humanity descends, as it did 75 or so years ago, into the abyss. In our final chapter, we discuss what needs to be done to stop fascism in the early 21$^{st}$ century.

# Fighting fascism

However bad the crisis, there is nothing inevitable about fascism. Germany between 1929 and 1933 saw the formation of the most powerful fascist movement in history. Yet even here, the Nazis might have been stopped but for the sectarian stupidity of the German Communist Party (KPD). Let us review this dismal record, for it is rich in lessons.

Hermann Remmele, a leading German Communist, summed up his party's viewpoint in the German Reichstag in October 1931:

> ...once they [the Nazis] are in power, the united front of the proletariat will emerge and make a clean sweep of everything... We are not afraid of the fascists. They will shoot their bolt quicker than any other government.

This was the official position. The German Communist Party was by this time a monolithic organisation that took its orders from Stalin. All members, high and low, were expected to peddle the same line. There was little room for independent thought, let alone open dissent. No-one survived for long as a party member in open defiance of the dominant theory of 'Social Fascism'.

According to the theory, the main enemy was not the Nazis (who won 6.4 million votes in 1930), but the Social Democrats (with 8.6 million votes). The Communists (4.6 million votes) spent most of their time attacking the Social Democrats, seeking to replace them as the main party of the German working class.

'The 14 September [the date of the 1930 general election] was the high-point of the Nazis' advance,' proclaimed the Communist Party's Berlin daily; '...what comes after can be only decline and fall.'

So complacent were the Communists – and so blinded by their hostility to the Social-Democrats – that they sometimes combined with the Nazis to attack meetings of workers hosted by their rivals. Here is a report – authored by a Communist activist – of one such attack in early 1921 on a social-democratic union conference of seamen and dockers:

> When the conference opened, the galleries were packed with 200 or 300 Communists and Nazis. I was in charge of operations for the Communists and Storm-troop leader Walter Tricow for the Nazis. In less than two minutes, we had agreed on a plan of action. As soon as the conference of the Social Democrats was under way, I got up and launched a harangue from the gallery. In another part of the hall, Tricow did the same...the chairman gave the order to eject the two troublemakers from the building... As soon as the first trade-union delegate touched one of us, our followers rose and bedlam started. The furniture was smashed, the participants beaten, the hall turned into a shambles...[1]

Though it seems almost inconceivable that a trade-union meeting should be broken up by an alliance of revolutionaries and fascists, the event was celebrated the following day in the Communist Party press, which reported that incensed workers had turned on their treacherous leaders and given them a thorough 'proletarian rub-down'.

The madness afflicted the KPD from top to bottom. In August 1931, for example, when the Nazis initiated a referendum in an attempt to overturn the discredited, right-wing, pro-austerity

SPD government of Prussia, the response of the Communists was to put conditions on their support and, when these were rejected, to campaign alongside the Nazis against the government in what they now described as a 'red referendum'.

The referendum was lost, but the Nazis raised their profile, gained popular support, and moved politics to the right. The KPD, on the other hand, had weakened itself and the labour movement by driving a wedge between the Communists and the SPD-supporting workers.

There is a direct parallel here with Brexit. Britain's EU referendum was an initiative of UKIP and the Tory Right. The Leave campaign was dominated by anti-migrant racism. To talk of 'Lexit' and 'People's Brexit' in this context is no different from the German Communists proclaiming the 1931 vote in Prussia to be a 'red referendum'. And the effect has been similar: to strengthen the Far Right and to drive a wedge between the Lexit Left and the mass of progressive workers and youth, who voted, with sound political instinct, Remain.

In the July 1932 general election, the Nazis got 13.7 million votes, 37% of the total, and became the largest party in the Reichstag. The combined vote of the workers' parties, the Social Democrats and the Communists, was slightly less, at 13.2 million (36%). So the Nazis had failed to 'decline and fall', as the Communist leadership had predicted. Despite this, the main enemy remained the 'Social Fascists'. As Communist leader Ernst Thälmann explained in September 1932:

> The Trotskyists put forward the slogan of unity of the SPD with the KPD to divert the desire for unity among the masses into fake political channels...precisely at the present stage in Germany the two [the SPD and the Nazis] appear in their true colours as 'twin brothers'...

Now it was no longer a matter of the Nazis having passed their peak. On the contrary, the Communists expected them to take power. But they would not last, and their brief rule would be but the prelude to socialist revolution. 'After Hitler, our turn,' proclaimed Thälmann.

Hitler came to power in January 1933. The Nazi dictatorship destroyed the German labour movement and went on to launch a world war and to murder millions in the death camps. It is possible – very possible – that had the Communists formed an alliance with the Social-Democrats to fight fascism in 1932, Hitler could have been stopped.[2]

Looking back on it now, the lunacy is obvious. How to explain it?

The SDP had engineered the defeat of the German Revolution between 1918 and 1923. The German Communists had been prone to 'ultra-leftism' ever since, remaining deeply hostile to the treacherous SDP leadership and unwilling to form united fronts with it in pursuit of common goals. But their sectarian instincts were reinforced by the line coming from Moscow.

The Comintern, the Moscow-based Communist International, had been set in the hope of turning the Russian Revolution into a world-wide socialist revolution. But when the revolutionary tide ebbed away, leaving backward, impoverished Russia isolated, the Bolshevik regime disintegrated. By the late 1920s, the Comintern had become a tool of Stalin and the new bureaucratic ruling class that had emerged from the wreckage of war and the decay of the revolutionary movement.[3]

Ultra-left sectarianism had become official Soviet policy as a cover for the counter-revolutionary character of the dramatic changes under way within Russia, where democracy had been destroyed, exploitation was intensifying in the factories, the peasants were losing their land, and the gulags were fast filling up.

These changes were masked by left rhetoric which insisted that a new revolutionary wave was rising – against all evidence to the contrary. Foreign communist parties were expected to comply – irrespective of their own judgement about the situation in their own countries. Precious few activists had any real understanding of what was happening in Russia. Stalin wore the mantle of the Bolshevik Revolution. Moscow was the red beacon lighting the way towards a new socialist order. When the Comintern ordered its constituent parties to attack the socialists – not the fascists – during this 'Third Period' phase (1928-1934), compliance was almost absolute.

In the fallout from the German catastrophe, Stalin flipped from the ultra-left madness of the 'Third Period' to the equally disastrous collaborationism of 'Popular Frontism'. Hitler was exceptionally hostile to the Soviet Union and intent on German expansion in Eastern Europe. The Soviet Union found itself imperilled by its diplomatic isolation, and Stalin now sought an accommodation with the Western powers. So revolutionary posturing was abandoned in favour of broad 'anti-fascist' alliances with all 'progressive forces'. This, in practice, meant suppressing revolutionary struggle. The result was another catastrophic defeat at the hands of fascism – in Spain, which became the main testing-ground for the popular-frontism now imposed upon the world's communist parties.

When the generals launched a military coup to overthrow the democratically elected Popular Front government in July 1936, the Communist leadership argued that the workers should leave matters to the authorities. This amounted to capitulation, since virtually the whole of the army supported Franco.

The workers took no notice. Revolution from below secured most of northern and eastern Spain, with workers' control of the factories, peasant land seizures, and the creation of popular militias.

In the militias, officers were elected, rank carried no privileges, and tactics were debated. Much had to be improvised, since the Nationalists began the war with most of the weapons. But the Republicans had one potentially decisive advantage: the appeal of their revolutionary message to ordinary soldiers conscripted to fight in the interests of officers, landlords, and priests. 'A civil war is waged...not only with military but also with political weapons,' explained Trotsky.

> From a purely military point of view, the Spanish Revolution is much weaker than its enemy. Its strength lies in its ability to rouse great masses to action. It can even take away the army from its reactionary officers. To accomplish this, it is only necessary to advance seriously and courageously the programme of the socialist revolution.
>
> It is necessary to proclaim that from now on the land, factories, and shops will pass from the hands of the capitalists into the hands of the people... The fascist army could not resist the influence of such a programme for 24 hours.

It was not to be. The Republican leaders were deeply hostile to the revolution. The Spanish Communist Party (PCE), true to the popular-front line dictated by Moscow, supported them. Socialist experiments were condemned as a threat to the alliance with the liberal bourgeoisie.

The PCE became increasingly powerful, partly because it bore the *imprimatur* of the Bolshevik Revolution, partly because workers were attracted to its radical-sounding rhetoric, partly because Stalin was supplying Russian military hardware. He who pays the piper calls the tune: communist guns meant communist influence.

But the PCE was a sinister counter-revolutionary force. Its slogan – 'first win the war, then win the revolution' – gulled workers with hope while justifying the disarming of the militias and the return of the factories to the capitalists and the land to the landlords.

In honour of Moscow's popular-frontist line, the PCE used its control of Russian arms to help the Republican government create a conventional Popular Army controlled from above that would defend private property.

In May 1937, the liberals and their Stalinist allies felt strong enough to go onto the offensive against the centre of the revolutionary movement: the city of Barcelona in Catalonia. The militias were provoked into action by government seizure of the telephone exchange. After five days of barricade fighting, however, the militia leaders gave up, allowing the city to be flooded with 5,000 counter-revolutionary 'Assault Guards'.

Savage repression followed. The POUM (the main revolutionary-socialist party) was made illegal. Its leaders were arrested, tortured, and murdered. The anarchist and POUM militias were forcibly incorporated into the Popular Army and put under regular military discipline. Dissidents were denounced as 'Trotsky-fascists'. Estates and factories were returned to their former owners.

The May 1937 counter-revolution crushed the spirit and potential of the popular revolution of July 1936. The Spanish Civil War was transformed from a revolutionary war between classes into a conventional war between rival fractions of the same class, one liberal, the other fascist.

The outcome was now determined by firepower, not politics. This meant victory for Franco, who was supported by Fascist Italy and Nazi Germany. Barcelona fell to fascism in January 1939, Madrid in March, confirming the truth of Trotsky's epitaph for the Spanish Revolution: 'The demand not to transgress the bounds of bourgeois democracy signifies in practice not a defence of the democratic revolution but a repudiation of it.'[4]

The triumph of fascism in Germany was facilitated by the ultra-left stupidity of a policy which divided the working class and drove a wedge between the revolutionary vanguard of the class and the majority of more moderate workers. The triumph of fascism in Spain was facilitated by the liberal stupidity of crushing a revolutionary movement capable of undercutting the cohesion of the hostile army by offering social emancipation to the peasant soldiers forming its rank-and-file. In both cases, the leadership of the Communist Party, acting under orders from Moscow, led the working class to total defeat.

It could have been otherwise. History is an open, contingent process; nothing is predetermined. The course of the future depends upon the choices we make in the present.

Let us consider an alternative approach to fighting fascism – one that works. Because we are writing mainly for a British readership, we take our two examples from British history, with a focus on two signal events: the defeat of the British Union of Fascists in 1934-36; and the defeat of the National Front in 1977-79.

## THE BATTLE OF CABLE STREET AND
## THE BRITISH COMMUNIST PARTY

Left activism in interwar Britain was dominated by the Communist Party (CP). Though by the 1930s it was no longer in fact a revolutionary party – it had degenerated under Stalinist leadership – it was still widely seen as such, and it was the natural home for working-class militants who wanted to fight poverty, fascism, and war.

The British CP never achieved the mass membership of its European counterparts. Throughout its history, it remained a fringe party. Nonetheless, in its heyday, it was several times larger than any of the British far-left groups of the recent past. Membership peaked at 12,000 at the time of the General Strike in 1926, collapsed to a low of less than 2,500 a few years later, but then, mainly due to united-front work around unemployment, rents, fascism, and solidarity with Spain through the dark years of the 1930s, slowly recovered, reaching 6,500 in 1935, 11,000 in 1936, and 18,000 in 1939. In the middle of the Second World War, party membership hit an all-time peak at around 50,000.

The party's struggle against fascism had begun as early as 1931, with disruption of meetings of Mosley's New Party, and then ramped up in 1933, when Mosley relaunched his movement as the British Union of Fascists (BUF). The clashes between Fascists and Communist-led protestors became increasingly violent as the BUF evolved into a more hard-line paramilitary and anti-semitic organisation.

The climax came with Mosley's decision in late 1936 to march through Stepney in London's East End. The BUF, whose violence and racism had led to its political marginalisation, was eager to build a strong working-class base and had poured resources into the East End, attracting a fair number of recruits, particularly in areas where the labour movement was weak. Stepney was home to a large proportion of East London's community of Jewish immigrants from Eastern Europe. Many of them were Communists. Mosley's decision to march through the heart of this community was deliberate provocation.

But the Communist Party leadership was now following Stalin's popular-front line. This meant forming alliances with liberals, courting respectability, and reining in the street politics. So the party's London District Committee called for a march from the Embankment to a rally in Trafalgar Square to coincide with the BUF march through the East End planned for 4 October. This triggered an internal crisis when it became clear that local activists were determined to defend their streets. Four days before the march, therefore, the CP leadership caved in and redirected their supporters to Aldgate.[5]

Stepney was in ferment. 'They shall not pass' became the rallying-cry of a vast anti-fascist movement of ordinary East Enders. Phil Piratin, a leading Communist activist, describes the preparations:

> Scores of meetings were held in all parts of London, but particularly East London... Thousands of posters, hundreds of thousands of leaflets, and hundreds of gallons of whitewash were employed in advertising the counter-demonstration. Approaches were made to trades councils, trade unions, and Labour parties to participate. Many did, in spite of the counter-propaganda put over by almost every other section of the movement. The Labour Party, the *Daily Herald*, the *News Chronicle*, the Jewish Board of Deputies, all appealed to the people to stay away.[6]

The BUF assembly point was Royal Mint Street. From there, three roads into the East End were open to them. All three had to be blocked; and the defence of the East End had to be co-ordinated between these three points, so a high level of organisation was necessary, with a 'headquarters' linked to the various 'fronts' by motor-cyclists and cyclists.

No-one knows how many people were on the streets that day. Estimates range from 20,000 to 200,000. That it was a mass mobilisation of local people is beyond dispute. It included the dockers, the Irish, and the Jews; the young and the old; women and men. The streets were cloaked in the red banners of the unions and the Left. The Jewish ex-Servicemen's Association marched around the borough advertising the counter-demonstration. Leman Street was blocked by trams, abandoned by their anti-fascist drivers. The streets shook with massed chants of 'They shall not pass!'

The police launched a series of attacks on the demonstrators, determined to smash a way through for the BUF. Cable Street, which gave its name to the battle, was the focus of the most ferocious fighting. Here the street was blocked by an overturned lorry, around which was piled old furniture, mattresses, and whatever else could be found. When the police charged the barricade, they were met by hails of bricks, stones, bottles, and marbles, both from the street and from upper-floor windows. Piratin describes the mood:

> Never was there such unity of all sections of the working class as was seen on the barricades at Cable Street. People whose lives were poles apart, though living within a few hundred yards of each other, bearded Orthodox Jews and rough-and-ready Irish Catholic dockers – these were the workers that the fascists were trying to stir up against each other.[7]

The police attacks failed. The police commissioner was forced to reroute the BUF march through the West End. Mosley's movement appeared weak and went into decline. Three months later, the government banned the wearing of uniforms and paramilitary organisation. Anti-semitism was driven to the political fringes. Communist Party membership soared and the labour movement as a whole gained in confidence.

The Communist Party did not restrict itself to fighting fascism. It had provided the leadership and much of the framework of the National Unemployed Workers Movement (NUWM) since the early 1920s. The NUWM aimed to organise the unemployed in both local struggles against means testing and cuts in relief and in high-profile 'hunger marches' to demand national action. In 1932, for example, when around 1,500 hunger marchers who had come all the way from Glasgow reached Hyde Park, they were joined by around 100,000 London trade unionists and socialists. The demonstrators were attacked by 2,600 regular police and 750 'specials' wielding batons. The workers fought back by tearing up railings and breaking branches off trees.

There seems little doubt that the BUF's attempt to build support among the unemployed hit a wall – because the Communist-led NUWM fixed the politics of the unemployed firmly on the side of the Left. This account of the activity of the Maryhill branch in Glasgow gives a flavour of how it was done:

> People coming in were getting cut off from benefit as a result of the means test and all the other anomalies that were introduced then. And their case was taken up and there was always somebody at the labour exchanges representing them...the NUWM was organising, fighting appeals against the decision when people's benefits were cut, even turning out when people had been evicted for arrears of rent, advertising the many demonstrations which were taking place in Glasgow – at least once a week, where anything from 5,000 to 20,000 people were turning up...[8]

Rent, of course, was a wider issue, of concern to both the unemployed and the employed working class. Housing became a major focus of struggle in the late 1930s, especially in the East End, where the Communist Party was again central to events. In response to 'decontrolled' rents – which could mean private landlords imposing increases of up to 25% – a rent strike begun in a run-down block of flats in Bethnal Green soon spread across the borough and into neighbouring Stepney. A landmark battle erupted in the summer of 1939, when the tenants in Langdale Mansions refused to pay the rent for 21 weeks and, supported by thousands of protestors, beat back attempts by bailiffs and police to evict them.

Victories were infectious. Rent reductions in one block encouraged dozens of other tenant groups to mount their own battles. And the example of the East End was followed elsewhere. By the time the Second World War broke out in September 1939, a wave of tenant struggles was sweeping Britain.

As with the struggle against unemployment, the economic struggle for cheaper housing intersected with the political struggle against fascism. Piratin reports a housing battle at Paragon Mansions in June 1937 that involved two families slated for eviction. In both cases, they were members of the BUF. But the Fascists had done nothing, whereas the Communists organised a successful campaign. Piratin continues:

> The news [of the victory] went around very quickly. The barricades came down and the 'ammunition' was disposed of. The lessons did not require being pressed home. BUF membership cards were destroyed voluntarily and in disgust...
>
> We were now supplementing our propaganda with positive action. The kind of people who would never come to our meetings, and had strange ideas about Communists and Jews, learned the facts overnight and learned the real meaning of the class struggle...[9]

The British Communist Party's struggle against interwar fascism is rich in lessons. Before we draw these out, however, we wish to describe a somewhat similar experience in the late 1970s. This will serve to confirm that the lessons of Cable Street are of general significance.

## LEWISHAM, ROCK AGAINST RACISM, AND THE ANTI-NAZI LEAGUE

The post-war boom had ended in 1973. Unemployment doubled. Wages were cut. Spending on housing, health, education, and welfare was slashed. A Labour government was responsible and its working class supporters lost faith. Britain's fascists, marginal since the 1930s, raised their heads.

The decline of empire and commonwealth immigration had already created a focus for far-right agitation. The tabloids regularly ran scare stories, the police force harassed black youth on the streets, and politicians ramped up the racism by passing laws to restrict immigration. Thus was the stage set, in the context of the 1970s crisis, for racism to become a major political force.

By the middle of the decade, the National Front (NF), an organisation founded by veteran neo-Nazis, was growing rapidly, attracting mainly working-class members and voters on the basis of virulent and often violent anti-black racism. Its membership seems to have peaked at just under 20,000, and the party secured 120,000 votes in the Greater London Council elections in May 1977. It seemed poised, therefore, to have a significant impact on the next general election, due to take place in 1979 at the latest, and was promising to stand in more than 300 constituencies. On the streets, there was a surge in fascist violence against minorities – 31 black people were murdered by racists between 1976 and 1981 – and in attacks on left-wing activists.[10]

In 1976, a group of young left-wing activists interested in music, many of them members of the International Socialists (soon to be renamed the Socialist Workers Party), launched Rock Against Racism (RAR).[11] They began issuing a counter-cultural magazine – *Temporary Hoarding* – aimed at disaffected youth, and set about organising music gigs with a radical, mainly anti-racist edge. At first it was a bit folksy and retro, but it soon established links with new bands, becoming a lively mix of punk, reggae, rock 'n' roll, soul, funk, and jazz. It eventually took off, not just as a mass youth counter-cultural phenomenon, but as an innovative and dynamic intervention in the music business, spawning new synthetic forms. RAR was anarchic, disruptive, and shocking, and this enabled it to connect with a wide layer of alienated youth and draw them towards anti-racist politics.

Critical to the success of RAR was that it was not controlled by the SWP leadership: it was never a party 'front' and it never followed a 'line'. RAR was a loose alliance of rank-and-file activists and music fans who acted as the catalyst of a movement that simply took off, with RAR gigs suddenly and spontaneously springing up all over the place.[12]

Meantime, events on the streets were taking an ugly turn. The police went on the rampage against black youth in the south London suburb of Lewisham, egged on by the tabloids, who had generated a moral panic around 'black mugging'. The Lewisham force launched what it called 'Operation PNH' – which some local activists believed stood for 'police nigger hunt'. Sixty black youngsters were arrested, 18 of whom were charged, and a local defence campaign was set up. The National Front then announced an 'anti-mugging' march through Lewisham for 13 August.

Two separate counter-mobilisations were called. One of these, led by a moderate alliance of councillors and clerics, was planned to end before the NF march began. The other, led by the SWP, aimed to confront the NF march head-on and attempt to stop it.

In the event, many of the people on the first march joined the second mobilisation, and this also attracted large numbers of local black youth. Around 6,000 anti-fascists took part in the counter-demonstration, which early on broke through police lines and cut the fascist march in two, and later prevented it reaching the centre of Lewisham by occupying the space and holding it against the police until the NF had dispersed. The police, in revenge, then launched an all-out attack on the anti-fascists.[13]

Lewisham, though on a smaller scale, had a significance similar to that of Cable Street 40 years before. As one anti-fascist activist put it:

Lewisham was our Cable Street. We had in mind the slogan from 1936, 'They shall not pass!' It was our generation's attempt to stop fascism. It was ragged, scrappy. It got bad publicity. But it was a real success. The NF had been stopped, and their ability to march through black areas had been completely smashed.[14]

Lewisham demoralised the fascist cadre, many of whom had been battered. They afterwards turned on their leaders for their failure to protect them. They would never march again in such numbers.

Despite the police violence, despite a media witch-hunt in the days afterwards, despite further bitter clashes over the next two years, the Left had denied the National Front control of the streets. David Widgery, an SWP activist and leading member of RAR, sums up the feelings engendered by the counter-mobilisation in words that echo those of Phil Piratin after Cable Street:

As the day became more brutal and frightening, and the police, furious at their failure, turned to take revenge on the counter-demonstrators, there was one big flash of recognition on the faces in the groups: between dread and socialist, between lesbian separatist and black parent, between *NME* speed-freak and ASTMS branch secretary. We were together... The mood was justly euphoric. Not only because of the sense of achievement – they didn't pass, not with any dignity anyway, and the

police completely lost the absolute control [they] had
boasted about – but also because, at last, we were all in
it together.[15]

The Battle of Lewisham – if that is not too grand a title – was
the springboard for the launch of the Anti-Nazi League (ANL).
The aim now was to build the broadest possible movement
against racism and fascism, and to use this movement to expose
the National Front as Nazis, to isolate them by mounting a mass
propaganda campaign to draw off soft support, and to mobilise
the numbers needed to prevent them meeting and marching.

The success of the ANL surpassed all expectations. Only the
Campaign for Nuclear Disarmament in the 1960s and the Stop
the War Coalition in the 2000s have matched it in scale in post-
war Britain. Between 1977 and 1979, nine million leaflets were
distributed and 750,000 badges sold. Around 250 ANL branches
were established, and up to 50,000 people counted themselves
members. Affiliates included 50 Labour parties and dozens of
trade-union branches, including engineering workers, miners,
transport workers, civil servants, journalists, teachers, and local-
government workers. RAR, working alongside the ANL, organised
300 gigs and five carnivals in 1978 alone. The largest carnivals
attracted 100,000 people. RAR and ANL badges were worn in
every school playground. Anti-racism became hegemonic.

The National Front was battered to pieces. Its membership collapsed to 10,000 in 1979. It then split in two amid
much rancour, and was down to less than 1,000 by 1985. NF
leader Martin Webster was in no doubt about the cause. Peter
Hain, one of the leaders of the ANL, took Webster to court for
libel in 1982 and there heard his firsthand testimony on the
demise of the Front:

He was still extremely bitter and remarkably candid.
The picture he gave, and he clearly believed it, was that
prior to 1977, the NF were unstoppable and he was well

on the way to becoming prime minister. Then suddenly the Anti-Nazi League was everywhere and knocking the sheer hell out of them. He said that the sheer presence of the ANL had made it impossible to get NF members onto the streets, had dashed recruitment, and cut away at their vote. It wasn't just the physical opposition to the marches; they had lost the propaganda war too.[16]

## ANTI-FASCIST STRATEGY

First is the deed. It is necessary to act, for only by acting may we change reality. One lesson of the struggle against fascism in Britain in both the 1930s and the 1970s is that arguments, meetings, and token protests are not enough. The struggle against fascism means direct action to protect minorities from attack and stop the fascists building a movement.

But this requires organisation and mass support. Both the East End Communists in the 1930s and the London SWP in the 1970s constituted sufficiently large and well-rooted activist networks to be able to mobilise large numbers of people in the anti-fascist struggle. The party networks functioned like small cogs at the heart of a machine. These turned medium-sized cogs – Labour parties, union branches, tenants associations, black groups, women's groups. And these in turn were connected to the largest cogs of all – the great masses of ordinary working-class people in the wider community.

But the working class is not an army following orders. The mechanism of mass mobilisation is fuelled by ideas. People must be persuaded to come out and fight. So the propaganda battle to expose the fascists, to explain the threat, to kindle a sense of solidarity, is vital. And this, moreover, needs to be linked to the wider struggle for economic betterment and social change.

It is not enough to condemn racism as morally wicked. It must be shown that united class struggle offers a real alternative, and that the fascists seek to divide working people in the face of their exploiters. The Communist Party undercut the appeal of the BUF by fighting unemployment and high rents in the 1930s. The SWP serviced a clutch of 'rank-and-file' groups in the unions, agitated in support of unofficial strikes, and had launched a Right to Work campaign in the mid 1970s before it launched the Anti-Nazi League in the late 1970s.

These lessons must be set against alternative anti-fascist strategies which historical experience has shown to be mistaken. These tend to recur in one form or another in every period. The matter is so urgent – the threat of fascism so immediate – that we feel bound to critique each of these alternatives in detail. We have boiled them down to six distinct arguments. Their misguided advocates we label 'capitulators', 'duckers', 'delusionals', 'liberals', 'liquorice allsorts', and 'squaddists'. In each case, we first provide a short summary of the argument, and then present our critique. At the end of the chapter, we present our six 'golden rules' of anti-fascist strategy.

## CAPITULATORS

> The basic argument: *The Left should respond to the concerns of people drawn to fascist arguments, especially over immigration, by adopting policies that acknowledge and address those concerns.*

This is often the argument of liberal and social-democratic politicians. There is a clamour around immigration, they say, and if we do not accommodate to it, we will be marginalised politically and the Far Right will become even stronger.

This is the opposite of the truth. If immigration controls are the answer, then the problem must be migration. Thus, instead of fighting fascism, liberals and social-democrats who argue for immigration controls simply reinforce the dominant far-right discourse. Instead of resisting the stampede to the right, they join it and increase its momentum.

If migrants are the problem, moreover, then perhaps the

people who are most forthright on this question are the most to be trusted to deal with it.

Again and again, we see concessions to racism by main-stream politicians ramping up support for the Far Right. We see it in Britain today. UKIP led the charge on immigration and Brexit (two issues which have become inseparable in modern British politics). The Tory Right, which joined the Leave campaign, echoed the racist rhetoric of UKIP. Moderate Tories, the Liberal Democrats, and New Labour, supporting the Remain campaign, insisted they too would be tough on immigration. Now we have Theresa May's Tory Government set upon a 'hard Brexit' because, as she explained in a keynote speech,

> In the last decade or so, we have seen record levels of net migration in Britain, and that sheer volume has put pressure on public services, like schools, stretched our infrastructure, especially housing, and put a downward pressure on wages for working-class people. As Home Secretary for six years, I know that you cannot control immigration overall when there is free movement to Britain from Europe.
>
> ...the message from the public before and during the referendum campaign was clear: Brexit must mean control of the number of people who come to Britain from Europe. And that is what we will deliver.[17]

May has no problem with blaming migrants for social distress rather than bankers. Liberals and social-democrats who then parrot the same line – like the New Labour careerists worried about their parliamentary seats – merely feed the right-wing mood that is slowly destroying their political base.

In the Gramscian war of position, a chain of influence is tugging the world towards fascism. On one end – increasingly confident and bullish – are the racists of the Far Right. They now have the whole of the mainstream Centre tumbling towards them, with conservative, liberal, and social-democratic politicians echoing their anti-migrant, anti-Muslim rhetoric – but without ever managing to sound quite as convincing as the fascists themselves.

You do not fight fascism by propagating its arguments. You fight fascism by saying loudly and clearly: *Migrants are not to blame. Muslims are not to blame. All migrants and refugees are welcome here. Free movement of people is a basic human right. Controlled borders and immigration police are inherently racist.*

You fight fascism by counter-posing an alternative explanation of the crisis – that the rich and the corporations are to blame – and by proposing united class struggle from below as the way forward. You place a left weight on the opposite end of the chain.

## DUCKERS

The basic argument: *The Left should focus on its key 'bread and butter' issues like jobs, wages, housing, and the NHS, and downplay or avoid difficult issues like immigration.*

This is often the argument of socialists who are reluctant to make concessions to racism, but who fear courting unpopularity by speaking out on issues like immigration controls. Let us avoid the clamour around dog-whistle, scapegoat politics we despise, the argument runs, and move the debate onto the Left's preferred terrain.

The argument has now infected much of the Labour Left. Corbyn is under attack on the question of immigration from the New Labour Right. Carwyn Jones, Labour's Welsh leader, for example, attacked him for refusing to join the anti-migrant chorus, saying, 'We have to be very careful we don't drive our supporters into the arms of UKIP.'[18]

Andy Burnham, the former Labour leadership contender, went much further, announcing that 'there is nothing socialist about open borders', that free movement has been 'defeated at the ballot-box and is no longer an option', and that 'our reluctance in confronting this [immigration] debate is undermining the cohesion of our communities and the safety of our streets'.[19]

The pressure on the chain – pulled by the Far Right – now extends all the way to Momentum, the 'Corbynista' movement inside the Labour Party. There has been no overt support for anti-migrant scapegoating or stronger immigration controls. But there has been 'accommodation' to the rightward pull on the question of racism. It takes two forms. One is silence. The line is: don't mention immigration. The other is imitation. The slogans of the Far Right are picked up and waved around with the font colour changed to red.

Thus, Momentum announced a series of nationwide events and debates to coincide with the Government's triggering of Article 50. The name for these events? 'Take Back Control' – the political slogan of the Leave campaign in the EU referendum campaign.

'Take Back Control will be about reclaiming the narrative and opening up the negotiations,' explained one of the organisers. 'This is our Brexit.'

But it is neither our slogan nor our Brexit: both are the territory of the Far Right. 'Take Back Control' – does it need spelling out? – was code for immigration controls during the EU referendum campaign.

Worse still is the claim from another of the organisers that Corbyn's re-election as Labour leader and Trump's election as American president 'are all part of a revolt against politics as usual'. He continued:

> Individuals have felt powerless for decades and are starting to reassert themselves. But taking back control is not the preserve of the Right. We want to see a Great Britain that takes power back from the economic elites Trump and Farage belong to.[20]

Individuals are not 'starting to reassert themselves' when they vote for a tax-dodging billionaire, a ranting racist, a misogynist and self-confessed abuser of women like Trump. The 63 million Americans who voted for this political psychopath were no more 'starting to reassert themselves' than the 12 million Germans who voted for Hitler in 1932.

To put Trump in the same sentence as Jeremy Corbyn is not only crass: it is very dangerous, since it conflates Right and Left, and spreads political confusion and disorientation.

Perhaps the worst of it is the reference to '*Great* Britain'. Chilling echoes here of 'Make America Great Again'.

The far-right programme centres on nationalism and racism. You cannot fight the tidal wave of reaction that is now sweeping across the world by parroting the slogans and adopting the ideas of the Left's most bitter enemies.

Racism is being leveraged by the Far Right: they are using the issue to skew the whole of politics in their favour. To duck it is a moral disgrace. It is to betray some of the most persecuted and oppressed people in society when they are under attack from the media, the police, and the fascists.

To duck is also politically stupid. It means ignoring the cancer of hatred and division eating through the working class and undermining its ability to fight back. To stay silent on racism, immigration controls, the rights of migrants and refugees, and the cardinal principle of free movement in the current climate is to abandon socialist principle.

## DELUSIONALS

> The basic argument: *What we are seeing is a global revolt against the elites, and the Left should seize the moment to put itself at the head of the popular anger, advance its own demands, and build a mass movement for socialist transformation.*

If only this were true. What we are actually seeing is a tidal wave of racism and reaction led by the Far Right. For sure, it is directed against the liberal parliamentary elites. So were the interwar movements of Mussolini, Hitler, and Franco. The difference between an 'anti-elite' movement of the revolutionary Left and an 'anti-elite' movement of the counter-revolutionary Right is, of course, the difference between life and death.

Two harsh realities – the weakness of the labour movement and the strength of popular racism – make the 'People's Brexit' being promoted by sections of the British Left a delusional fantasy.

Without naming names, let me refer to one example among many, taken more or less at random from among the websites of the Left. In an article headed 'Next stop...the People's Brexit', we are told,

> We need to fight for an outcome that ensures a solution to the NHS funding crisis, a solution to the housing crisis, a raising of workers' wages and employment rights, as well as total opposition to scapegoating of migrants and racism in all its forms. In other words, for what Jeremy Corbyn has called a 'People's Brexit', a chance to shape the future of British society along egalitarian lines.[21]

So, in response to the wave of racism and reaction represented by the Brexit vote, and notwithstanding the perilous weakness of working-class organisation and consciousness, we are invited to content ourselves with holding up a picture of socialist transformation.

This is worse than delusional: it is deeply dangerous in a manner directly comparable with the politics of the world communist movement in the early 1930s. It is to imply that the Brexit vote was a left-wing assault on a corrupt neoliberal elite. It is to imply that our side is strong, that it is advancing, that it is poised to make great gains. It is to deny a clear and present danger. It is the sectarian stupidity of 'Third Period' Stalinism repackaged.

There is an urgent need to construct a defensive shield to protect the minorities, the migrants, and the labour movement; a defensive shield to block and begin to push back the racists. We need a united front of the workers, the youth, and the oppressed to challenge the growing normalisation of racism, to counter the abuse being hurled at the victims of the system, and to resist an increasingly repressive and racist state-machine.

## LIBERALS

The basic argument: *The Left should seek a 'progressive alliance' of all political parties opposed to racism and fascism.*

It seems obvious. Let us unite all progressive forces willing to make a stand against the advance of the Far Right. Let us maximise our chances of winning at the ballot-box by bringing everyone into the same electorate bloc and thus avoid splitting the vote.

But life is never so simple. Guardianista calls for a 'progressive alliance' are simply warmed-up interwar Popular Frontism. The fatal flaw with the Stalinist policy of the mid to late 1930s was that it *subordinated* the working-class movement to the liberal and social democratic politics of prospective centrist allies. The liberals and social-democrats were imposing austerity in Depression-era Europe. They were defending the rights of property when the unemployed were starving. They were pillars of a bankrupt economic system and a failed political system.

Does this sound familiar? Is it not the case that today's political elite – Tory, Liberal-Democrat, and New Labour – has merged into a uniform neoliberal technocracy promoting corporate power, privatisation, and austerity? Is it not the case that they have presided over a system of grotesque greed at the top and stagnation and squalor at the base that has provided the Far Right with its social base? And is it not also the case that many of these 'progressive' politicians have been echoing the racism they profess to deplore?

An alliance with Liberal Democrats and New Labour would be an alliance with the living dead. It would mean an alliance with neoliberal mantras and a politics corrupted by corporate interests. It would mean abandoning the struggle for an alternative economic strategy.

To fight racism and fascism, you have to offer an alternative. You have to argue for: the nationalisation of banking and money; the repudiation of the speculators' debts; a public takeover of property registered in tax-havens; big cuts in military expenditure; big rises in taxes on the rich and the corporations; a massive programme of public works; reversal of all NHS privatisation; abolition of casual labour; doubling of the minimum wage; repeal of all anti-union laws; and much more in the same vein. You have to argue for a radical alternative that will benefit the many at the expense of the few; you have to champion the 90% by taking on the wealth and power of the 1%. Only thus – with big, radical, ambitious proposals – with solutions on a scale to match the gravity of the crisis – can you hope to undercut the long-term appeal of the Far Right.

That is not all. You cannot allow effective anti-fascist action to be hamstrung by right-wing allies. Virtually the entire political Establishment opposed the Communist-led mobilisation at Cable Street: yet this was the decisive battle of the struggle against fascism in interwar Britain. Virtually the entire political Establishment denounced the SWP-led mobilisation at Lewisham: yet this shattered the morale of the fascist cadre, provided the launch pad for the ANL, and began the two-year process that smashed the National Front in the late 1970s. We cannot afford to subordinate the strategy and tactics of the struggle against fascism to the stupidity of liberals and social-democrats.

So we should not seek a 'progressive alliance' that involves ditching radical policies and militant tactics to appease lukewarm allies. Now let us be clear what we are *not* arguing: we favour a united front against fascism of the broadest possible coalition of forces. The Stop Trump Coalition (STC) – just launched as we complete this text – extends all the way from the Far Left to the Liberal Democrats. We welcome that: the broader the spectrum, the greater the number we can reach. But all constituents of the STC retain their political independence and remain free to argue about policies and tactics. This is quite different from a formal alliance with right-wing forces – a 'Popular Front' or 'progressive alliance' – that involves reducing matters to the lowest-common-denominator politics necessary to accommodate the most 'moderate' leaders.

The aim is united mass struggle from below – a movement of ordinary people, in the workplaces and colleges, on the estates and the streets, fighting racism and sexism, austerity and poverty, fascism and war. No-one is excluded. Everyone is welcome. No conditions are placed on joining the struggle. Social-democrats, liberals, even conservatives may choose to join an anti-fascist demonstration. But these forces cannot be allowed to suffocate the democracy and activity of the mass movement on the streets.

## LIQUORICE ALLSORTS

> The basic argument: *The Left should foster a spontaneous mushroom growth of grassroots activism by respecting the autonomy and choices of separate groups, by recognising the 'intersectionality' of the movement, and by avoiding the imposition of top-down theory and organisational hierarchy.*

We hope this is an accurate summary of the basic 'autonomist' argument. We do not wish to caricature it, but we find it difficult to give it coherent definition. It is, by its very nature, hard to tie down.

Everyone can agree that oppressed people should organise, mobilise, and fight back, not least in the struggle against racism and fascism. There is, of course, a long history of such struggles. Black power, women's liberation, and gay rights were central to the great upsurge of radical struggle between 1968 and 1975. Often enough, a section of the oppressed moves into action first, lighting a beacon, kindling a mood, and others, including the massed ranks of organised labour, followed behind. In Britain, students fighting on a range of issues, from the Vietnam War to authoritarian power-structures in the universities, dominated the struggle in 1968, but it was the mass strikes of industrial workers, especially the dockers and the miners, that broke the back of the 1970-74 Tory Government and eventually brought it down.

The problem that concerns us here is an autonomist movement that makes a virtue of difference, that actively favours separation, that sees 'intersectionality' as the centre of gravity for radical politics.

This is compounded by a 'neoliberalisation' of political activism, where it becomes a simple matter of individual choice which issue one campaigns on, which group one joins, which struggle one prioritises.

But the class struggle is not like shopping. History is not a market-place shaped by consumer choice. We do not choose whether racism is rampant or fascism a threat. And therefore, since politics is not a game, since radical activism is a serious matter, we cannot reduce it to personal preference.

Autonomism and intersectionality have become an epidemic because they have lodged themselves in the neoliberal substrate we analysed in Chapter 4. They are the distorted radicalism of an era of defeat and retreat, of the hollow society and the political void, of atomisation, alienation, and anomie. They have flourished amid the decay of the traditions of solidarity and collective action that are, throughout history, the very essence of mass struggle from below. They are the rationale of small groups content to do their own thing in a corner.

The historical record is unequivocal: the oppressed advance and retreat together. Unity and solidarity are the basis of successful struggle, the strong give inspiration to the weak, and victories on one front lead to victories on others. The black Civil Rights Movement in the southern states in the early 60s inspired the Black Power Movement in the northern states in the late 60s. The black struggle inspired the students, the women, and the gays to fight. All these struggles fed into the anti-war movement, which, in combination with the struggle of a peasant-guerrilla army on the other side of the world, brought US imperialism to its greatest defeat, in Vietnam in 1973.

We support the self-organisation and self-defence of the oppressed. We support all struggles against exploitation, oppression, and violence. But we oppose separation and division within the movement. We oppose a 'liquorice allsorts' approach to politics, where anything goes, where difference becomes an organising principle, where everyone is free to choose their own priorities, where there is no proper perspective and strategy.

## SQUADDISTS

> The basic argument: *Because fascism is a mortal threat to all of us, whenever it arises, in whatever form, the Left must prioritise self-defence, confrontation, and physical attacks on fascist organisation to prevent it becoming rooted.*

The term 'squaddist' was coined in the early 1980s, when some anti-fascists, disappointed by the winding down of the Anti-Nazi League, organised themselves in separate groups with the explicit purpose of continuing a campaign of physical confrontation with the remnants of the National Front (and its small but more violent offshoot, the British Movement).

The ANL was wound down because the NF had been broken by the middle of 1979. Fascism ceased to have a mass form, and the anti-fascist movement therefore ebbed away. To continue a physical struggle in these circumstances meant seeking out individual fascists or small groups of fascists and beating them up. And since only small numbers of anti-fascists were involved, they ran they risk that they would end up getting beaten, or that they would be arrested and perhaps fined or even imprisoned. In December 1981, for example, eight anti-fascists from Manchester were jailed for between 6 and 15 months for possession of offensive weapons.[22]

This was helping no-one. The experience of such violence – against individuals, in a dark place – was squalid and demoralising. The effort and risk were unwarranted – because the fascists had ceased to be a serious threat, and the priority now was to organise resistance to the new Thatcher Government, which, backed by the full power of the state, was mounting a frontal assault on the British labour movement. In any case, reduced to the level of small-group confrontation, the advantage lay with the residual fascist hard-core, many of whom relished violence. Unsurprisingly, anti-fascist activists caught up in this netherworld of backstreet punch-ups degenerated politically; sometimes, in an atmosphere of drink and sexism, things were said among them that any socialist should be ashamed of.[23]

The essence of all socialist politics – anti-fascism is no exception – is that we seek to unite, organise, and mobilise the mass of ordinary people in active struggle in defence of their interests. Squaddism is the opposite of this.

## THE SIX GOLDEN RULES OF ANTI-FASCIST ACTION

Here, finally, we offer our summary prescription for an effective strategy for fighting fascism.

1. Mass campaigns of propaganda – with festivals, gigs, rallies, meetings, stalls, street theatre, banner drops, stunts, and protests – using badges, placards, leaflets, broadsheets, web articles, Facebook posts, Twitter tweets, and YouTube videos – are necessary to label and expose the fascists, to drain away their soft support, to isolate the hard core, and to mobilise active resistance.

2. Uncompromising adherence to anti-racist principles is essential to unite the oppressed, to rally our forces, and to erect a bulwark against the reactionary tide. The anti-fascist movement must say: *Migrants are not to blame. Muslims are not to blame. All migrants and refugees are welcome here. Free movement of people is a basic human right. Controlled borders and immigration police are inherently racist.*

3. Mass mobilisation of active anti-fascist forces is necessary to physically confront fascist organisations, to prevent them meeting, marching, campaigning, and organising, and to protect the minorities they target and the wider labour movement they threaten.

4. The largest possible numbers, drawn from the broadest possible range of organisations and campaigns, should be united

in the anti-fascist movement. But this must be an anti-fascist united front of radical forces, committed to effective action, not a 'progressive alliance' with the living dead based on lowest-common-denominator, do-nothing, dead-end politics.

5. The anti-fascist movement should advance radical alternative solutions to society's problems and give solidarity to all struggles for progressive social change. But it should not make support for some sort of 'programme' or 'line' a condition for active involvement in the anti-fascist struggle.

6. The anti-fascist movement should not be highly centralised or controlled from above. It should not preach a 'line' or lay down policy. It should encourage spontaneity and self-activity. It should be a loose alliance of local groups united in purpose, democratic in spirit, independent in action.

These are the golden rules – tried and tested in the great battles of the past. The aim is to smash fascism – the creeping fascism of Brexit, Trump, Le Pen, Wilders, Jobbik, and Golden Dawn.

We do not like violence. We oppose the violence of the militarised state, the violence of fascists, the violence of the cops. We also oppose the one-on-one backstreet violence of the squaddist. But we defend the right of the oppressed to self-defence, and we defend the right of the common people as a whole to defend themselves against the threat of fascism.

The policy of 'no platform' has occasionally become farcical. You cannot impose 'no platform' on anyone or anything if you are a mere handful: you require the mass collective force of the community as a whole to make it effective. But 'no platform' for fascism must indeed be the objective – for compelling moral, democratic, and political reasons.

We have a moral obligation to defend the oppressed against fascist violence and intimidation. The link between fascist activity – and racism more generally – and spikes in attacks on minorities is so well established it needs no further demonstration. No platform is about protecting vulnerable communities against violence, intimidation, and fear.

We have a democratic right to defend our freedoms – civil and political – against those who would destroy them. Those who deny democratic rights to the oppressed today, those who would deny them to all of us tomorrow, lose their own entitlement to freedom of expression.

We have a political imperative to prevent the destruction of the labour movement and the subjugation of the working class to the untrammelled dictatorship of capital and the state. The fascists crushed the skulls of the European working class under a terrific tank in the 1930s. They gave us Stalingrad, Auschwitz, and 60 million dead.

Never again! We must smash them – by any means necessary – before they smash us.

# Twelve theses on creeping fascism

Our argument in this book is that interwar fascism – what might be called 'first wave' fascism – has been caricatured and misinterpreted. Accordingly, we have attempted to broaden the historical perspective and, in the light of what we trust is a more comprehensive view, to revise the classical Marxist theory of fascism. In doing this, we have also drawn upon contemporary experience – that of fascism's 'second wave'. This appears to affirm the revised analysis; indeed, with each day that passes, the affirmation seems more emphatic.

Here we present the basic building blocks of our analysis in the form of 12 theses. We must acknowledge a debt to Michael Löwy, who has revived this method of presenting a Marxist argument with his 'Ten theses on the Far Right in Europe'.[1] Though we agree with much of his analysis, our emphasis is different enough to warrant an alternative list. We have, however, indicated in the footnotes where we feel there is significant correspondence between his theses and ours.

## 1. A CONTEXT OF WORLD CAPITALIST CRISIS

Fascism becomes a mass force in the context of capitalist crisis. The crisis today is a slow social malaise rather than an abrupt economic collapse. The bubble economy, the hollow society, and the political void – and the atomisation, alienation, and anomie of individual experience – provide the context for fascist growth.[2]

## 2. POLARISATION AROUND NATIONALIST MYTH

Fascism involves political polarisation around the concept of the nation-state and the historic myths of nationalism – and, by extension, around associated ideas of cultural racism/exclusion, sexism/the family/the social order, and authoritarianism. Key features of second-wave fascism are economic nationalism, Islamophobia, anti-migrant racism, and moral panics around terrorism, law and order, community cohesion, and traditional values.[3]

## 3. THE THREAT OF REVOLUTION FROM BELOW

Neoliberal capitalism is pregnant with the possibility of new popular revolts from below. The threat to the system is evident in successive waves of mass struggle since 1999 – the anti-capitalist, anti-war, and anti-austerity movements. The continued rule of the rich and the corporations cannot be guaranteed. The system requires ideological and political mechanisms for containing and canalising the social discontent generated by a long-term crisis of stagnation-slump to which it has no solution.

## 4. AN ACCUMULATION OF HUMAN DUST

Fascism is not a direct reflection of class interests, whether of big capital, the middle class, or the 'left behind' working class. It does not embody the political programme of any distinct social group. It represents an accumulation of human dust – of individuals acting not on a class basis but as formless social detritus cast adrift by the capitalist crisis – and cohering into a political force around the reactionary myths of nation, race, and gender.[4]

## 5. A MOVEMENT OF PROCESS AND ACTION
Fascism is not a thing, but a motion; not a fixed form, but a continuous process of becoming. It evolves historically in the concrete circumstances of a particular historical conjuncture, and in interaction and collision with other social and political forces. It cannot, therefore, be defined in relation to a check-list of standardised fascist characteristics: it must be understood in terms of its inner essence – a political movement formed of human dust to achieve a mythic 'national regeneration' – and the historical dynamic to which this essence gives rise.[5]

## 6. A SPECTRUM OF EVOLVING FORMS
Fascism cannot be sharply distinguished from far-right 'populism' or even traditional conservatism. The Far Right is best understood as a spectrum of forms in a state of flux. Any particular organisational expression of what might be called 'the fascist essence' has the capacity to evolve in different ways according to circumstances. The trend of global politics in the last 35 years has been to the right. We appear to have arrived at a second tipping point in that journey, the election of Trump marking a qualitative shift, much as the elections of Thatcher and Reagan did in 1979/1980. Our current trajectory is towards harder, more extreme, more 'fascist' forms of right-wing politics.[6]

## 7. THE STATE AS INSTRUMENT OF REPRESSION
Fascist paramilitaries have always played a secondary role. This was true even in the most extreme cases – in Italy in 1922 and Germany in 1933 – and was certainly true of other interwar fascisms. The existing state-apparatus was always the primary instrument of repression, dictatorship, and totalitarianism. With a less abrupt, visceral, and polarised crisis today, the role of fascist paramilitaries is even less prominent. Trump has no need of Brownshirts when he controls the US police, judiciary, and prison system.

## 8. THE CHANGING BALANCE OF CLASS FORCES

Fascism aims at a radical shift in the balance of class forces in favour of capital. The ways in which this is achieved include: weakening or destroying labour organisation; using police power to crush other forms of dissent; stimulating the economy with public works, state contracts, and protective tariffs; increasing military spending; using military power to advance the interests of corporations; and subordinating social life as a whole to 'national regeneration' (i.e. national capital-accumulation).

## 9. METHOD IN THE MADNESS

Fascism is contradictory and opportunistic. It appeals to passions rather than reason. Fascist leaders are usually socially maladjusted and sometimes clinically psychotic. This does not mean that fascism lacks a rational core. Nazi Germany pursued a state-capitalist economic policy that ended unemployment in the 1930s, and then pursued a war of imperial expansion that was clearly in the interests of German capital and was at first highly successful. The economic nationalism of today's Far Right is a rational response – from the perspective of capital – to the long-term crisis of stagnation-slump afflicting the neoliberal global order. Trump's rapprochement with Moscow, his hostility to Beijing, and his consequent pivot from Europe to the Pacific, is a rational extension of his economic nationalism.[7]

## 10. A DESPERATE DEFENSIVE BATTLE

Despite three great upsurges of protest against capitalism, war, and austerity within the last two decades, the neoliberal counter-revolution has continued to advance, rolling back virtually all the gains of the international working class in the post-war period. Though the possibility exists for new upsurges of mass struggle, the resistance of the labour and social movements is at present limited. It is necessary to recognise that we are, for the time being, engaged in a desperate, defensive, rearguard action, that we face the clear and present danger of fascism, and that we must adopt strategies of resistance and resurgence appropriate to the circumstances. *The Right is advancing. The Left is in crisis. Fascism threatens. Sound the alarm!*[8]

## 11. A MOVEMENT IN CONTRADICTION

Because fascism is highly contradictory, it is vulnerable to derailment and disintegration in the face of determined opposition. Three contradictions stand out: between its respectable image and its fascist essence ('suits or boots'); between its disruptive radicalism and both the workings of the existing state and the imperatives of capital accumulation ('fascists and conservatives'); between fascist leaders who want to run the system and fascist supporters who want to change it ('leaders and street-fighters'). Fascism is an amalgam of human dust held together by myth and false promise. It is an amalgam that can be shattered.

## 12. A MORTAL THREAT THAT CAN BE BEATEN

Fascism can be beaten. The vital ingredients of successful anti-fascist strategy are these: mass campaigning to expose and isolate the fascist core; uncompromising adherence to anti-racist principle (and progressive principles in general); mass mobilisation to deny fascism a platform; a big, broad, bold anti-fascist movement that aims to unite the largest possible number in effective action; support for radical alternative solutions to the crisis and for all forms of popular resistance; an anti-fascist movement that is united in purpose but loose in structure and democratic in form.[9]

# The struggle for the future

## THE FIRST FEW DAYS:
## THIS IS WHAT CREEPING FASCISM LOOKS LIKE

The composition of the new White House regime, and its actions during Trump's first ten days, confirm our 'creeping fascism' analysis. The personnel span the spectrum from Alt-Righters like Chief Strategist Steve Bannon to hard-right traditional Republicans like Vice-President Mike Pence (see list 'Trump personnel'). A battery of executive orders, interspersed with brazen lying and Twitter abuse, has confirmed the regime's determination to implement a roll-back, reactionary-racist programme without parallel in American history (see list 'Trump actions').

Naomi Klein is right to argue that Trump's 'crony cabinet' represents a corporate takeover of US government by vested interests under threat from popular protest:

> ...rather than risk the possibility of further progress, this gang of fossil-fuel mouthpieces, junk-food peddlers, and predatory lenders have come together to take over the government and protect their ill-gotten wealth... They are cutting out the middleman and doing what every top dog does when they want something done right – they are doing it themselves... After decades of privatising the state in bits and pieces, they decided to just go for the government itself. Neoliberalism's final frontier.[1]

She is right to argue that powerful, scheming, coldly-calculating corporate interests are at work. That we should not mistake the appearance – a narcissistic bully drunk on power – for the substance. The hard men of globalised capital are inside the White House alongside the racists, misogynists, and red-baiters.

And therefore there is method in the madness. Mussolini and Hitler were as ludicrous as Trump. But they personified a programme of national-capitalist regeneration and expansion that was wholly rational for their corporate backers. So it is with the neo-fascists in the White House.

Trump's economic nationalism is a response to the failure of neoliberal globalisation to end the long-term crisis of stagnation-slump that has afflicted the system since the 1970s and intensified since 2008. 'America First' protectionism may provoke retaliation, raise costs, and damage US capital. But capitalism is a contradictory system, so economic nationalism can also benefit capital, especially if it is supplemented – as it is being – with a programme of deregulation, tax cuts, government contracts, union busting, and a combination of economic and military threats against foreign competitors. The rapprochement with Russia and posturing against China is part of that – the beginning of a trade war that could one day become a nuclear-armed shooting war.

What of the racism and sexism, the attacks on migrants, the ban on Muslims, the threat to abortion rights, the baiting of journalists and dissidents? This, too, in the twisted logic of creeping fascism, has its own rationale: it is meat thrown to the lynch-mob, to appease it, soak up its aggression, and distract it from the real causes of social distress.

It is this, of course, that gives the regime its fascist flavour: the existence of an actual and potential mass movement assembled around the myths of nation, race, and family. We caught a glimpse of it on Friday 27 January, the week following the huge anti-Trump women's marches, when tens of thousands of 'pro-life' demonstrators marched in Washington against abortion rights, with Trump tweeting support, and Vice-President Mike Pence addressing the rally and proclaiming that 'life is winning again in America'.[2]

All this, surely, is what the beginning of fascism looks like in early 21st century America.

———————

## TRUMP PERSONNEL[3]

### VICE-PRESIDENT
### MIKE PENCE

A fundamentalist Christian who is anti-gay and anti-abortion. Once suggested HIV-prevention funding be reduced to fund 'gay cure' therapy. Signed Indiana's Religious Freedom Restoration Act allowing businesses to discriminate against gay people on religious grounds.

### ATTORNEY-GENERAL
### JEFF SESSIONS

A white-supremacist from Alabama who was denied judicial appointment for making racist remarks. Noted for saying he thought the Ku Klux Klan 'okay', until he learned that they smoked marijuana, for using the word 'nigger', and for declaring that the National Association for the Advancement of Coloured People and the American Civil Liberties Union were 'un-American'.

### CHIEF STRATEGIST AND SENIOR COUNSELOR
### STEVE BANNON

A former Goldman Sachs banker and former owner of far-right media outlet Breitbart News, which he says offers a platform for the Alt-Right. Was once charged with abusing his ex-wife. She later dropped charges, allegedly under duress from Bannon.

NATIONAL SECURITY ADVISOR
LIEUTENANT-GENERAL HERBERT MCMASTER
A hasty replacement for disgraced first choice for the post, Lieutenant-General Michael Flynn, McMaster is a military hawk, firmly anti-Russian and in favour of escalating the War on Terror, saying, 'I think it's okay for us to want to win against these misogynistic, murderous bastards in the greater Middle East.'

DEFENCE SECRETARY
GENERAL 'MAD DOG' JAMES MATTIS
A key commander in Afghanistan and Iraq, he played a major role in the butchery at the Battle of Fallujah. Statements include: 'It's a hell of a hoot. It's fun to shoot some people. I'll be right up there with you. I like brawling'; and 'Do not cross us. Because if you do, the survivors will write about what we do here for 10,000 years.'

TREASURY SECRETARY
STEVEN MNUCHIN
A $400 million net-worth banker who made a killing by aggressively pushing foreclosures during the Credit Crunch as CEO of OneWest Bank, evicting tens of thousands from their homes.

SECRETARY OF STATE
REX TILLERSON
Former CEO of Exxon who said of climate change: 'The world is going to have to continue using fossil fuels, whether they like it or not.' Asked whether Putin was a war criminal based on his targeting of civilians in Syria, he answered, 'I would not use that term.'

INTERIOR SECRETARY
RYAN ZINKE
Now responsible for managing public lands and waters, yet as Montana congressman he proposed cutting protections of public lands and waters.

## ENERGY SECRETARY
## RICK PERRY
A climate-change denier who wants to abolish his new department as well as the Environmental Protection Agency.

## LABOUR SECRETARY
## ANDREW PUZDER
Head of a big fast-food franchise, he opposes trade unions, any minimum wage, and industry regulations. In the past has attacked the Labour Department he now leads for being too pro-worker.

## HOUSING SECRETARY
## BEN CARSON
A retired neurosurgeon with no experience in urban development. He opposes programs to help homeowners, not least those with low incomes. He opposes racial equality legislation, considering it counterproductive.

## EDUCATION SECRETARY
## BETSY DEVOS
She opposes public schools and supports private Christian schools, an agenda she pushed in Michigan.

## HEALTH SECRETARY
## TOM RICE
He despises ObamaCare and intends to end it.

---

## TRUMP ACTIONS[4]

19 JANUARY
Cuts in funding announced for:
– Department of Justice's Violence Against Women programmes
– National Endowment for the Arts
– National Endowment for the Humanities

- Corporation for Public Broadcasting
- Minority Business Development Agency
- Economic Development Administration
- International Trade Administration
- Manufacturing Extension Partnership
- Office of Community Oriented Policing Services
- Legal Services Corporation
- Department of Justice's Civil Rights Division
- Department of Justice's Environmental and Natural Resources Division
- Overseas Private Investment Corporation
- UN Intergovernmental Panel on Climate Change
- Office of Electricity Deliverability and Energy Reliability
- Office of Energy Efficiency and Renewable Energy
- Office of Fossil Energy

## 20 JANUARY
- All regulatory powers of all federal agencies frozen.
- National Parks Service to stop using social media after RTing side-by-side photos of crowds for 2009 and 2017 inaugurations.
- About 230 protestors arrested in Washington DC at anti-Trump protests face unprecedented felony riot charges, including legal observers, journalists, and medics.
- Member of International Workers of the World union in critical condition after being shot in stomach at anti-fascist protest in Seattle.

## 21 JANUARY
- Trump brings 40 cheerleaders to meeting with CIA to cheer him during speech attacking media.
- White House press secretary Sean Spicer holds press conference to deny accuracy of media reports on relative size of Trump inauguration crowd, claiming largest attendance in history 'period'.

## 22 JANUARY
– White House advisor Kellyann Conway defends Spicer's lies as 'alternative facts' on national TV.
– Trump appears to blow kiss to director James Comey during meeting with FBI, then makes open-arms gesture, then hugs him.

## 23 JANUARY
– Trump reinstates global gag order which defunds international organisations that mention abortion.
– Spicer says US will not tolerate China's expansion onto islands in South China Sea, effectively threatening war with China.
– Trump repeats lie that between 3 and 5 million 'illegal' votes cost him popular vote in presidential election.
– Announcement that man who shot anti-fascist protester in Seattle released without charge.

## 24 JANUARY
– Spicer reiterates lie about 3 to 5 million 'illegal' voters.
– Trump tweets announcement that photo will hang in White House press room and claims it depicts inauguration-day crowd on 20 January (though it actually depicts women's march on 21 January).
– Environmental Protection Agency ordered to stop communicating with public through media and to freeze all grants and contracts.
– Department of Agriculture ordered to stop communicating with public through media and to stop publishing research – all communication henceforward to be authorised and vetted by White House.
– 'HR7' bill to prohibit federal funding of any health insurance, including ObamaCare/Medicaid, that includes abortion services goes to Congress for vote.
– Director of Department of Health and Human Service nominee Tom Price characterises federal guidelines on transgender equality as 'absurd'.

– Trump orders resumption of construction on Dakota Access Pipeline.
– North Dakota state congress considers bill to legalise killing protestors with cars if on roadways.
– Revealed that police had searched mobiles confiscated from demonstrators arrested at anti-Trump protests on inauguration day and accessed confidential information concerning lawyers' clients and journalists' sources.

25 JANUARY
– Trump orders construction of wall along US-Mexican border to begin.
– Trump announces ban on Muslims from seven countries (Iran, Iraq, Libya, Somalia, Sudan, Syria, Yemen) entering US.

———————

**A NEW MOVEMENT RISING?**
It was vast. You knew as you approached it. You saw people on the tube and the pavements with placards and banners. As you got closer, you found the street was rammed. The back of the march had not left Grosvenor Square when the rally started in Trafalgar Square. It was that big.

Facebook said around 35,000 were going and another 35,000 were 'interested' (whatever that means). The *Mirror* (which backed the demo) was reporting 100,000 on the day. Wherever that figure came from – the cops? – it was a gross underestimate. It could easily have been a quarter of a million.

This was London, 21 January 2017, the day after the crowning of the comb-over pig in the US capital – the 'Women's March on London'. More than half the marchers were young women. Many carried homemade placards. The messages were angry, funny, clever, imaginative, often all at once. The march was loud, buoyant, confident. The white tapes were snapped and the crowd surged across to fill the street. This was not some dreadful dirge on the passing of an era, with its escort of ageing veterans selling stale newspapers. It looked and sounded like it might be the dawning of a new mass movement of the Left.

Reports from Washington suggest the number there was at least a million. The pictures show the size of our side's mobilisation on the Saturday dwarfing that of Trump's supporters the day before at the inauguration. The new regime in the White House, stung by the comparison, took the trouble to issue a long press statement disputing what is blindingly obvious from the photos. We would expect nothing else. This is, after all, a 'fake news/post-fact/alternative fact' regime.

Similar marches took place in New York, Philadelphia, Chicago, and Los Angeles, and in an estimated 700 cities across the world. The women of the world had moved into action to protest the farce to which American democracy has been reduced when a bragging misogynist, a racist bigot, a bullying narcissist is elected to the presidency.

And then, barely a week later, a second explosion of protest rocked the States and again spilled across the world, this time protesting the travel ban on Muslims from seven named countries. Tens of thousands of protestors blockaded airport lounges across the US, each protest a carnival celebration of youth, diversity, and internationalism, each representing an alternative polar-opposite vision of America to that of the bigots in the White House.

But this is a 'shock and awe' regime. Each provocation is designed to shift the conversation to the right, to stampede the centre-ground into desperate concessions, to stir the passions of Trump's reactionary social-base. And the Far Right everywhere is relishing the moment. While the world's women marched on 21 January, Le Pen, Wilders, and other European far-right leaders were meeting in Koblenz in Germany, proclaiming 'the end of one world and the birth of a new'. Marine Le Pen heralded Brexit as stage one and Trump as stage two in a global far-right surge that may next see her take the French presidency.

The battle-lines of what looks set to become a massive,

world-wide, multi-front struggle to define an entire epoch are forming. On one side are the workers, the women, and the minorities, representing the age-old fight for equality, democracy, peace, and internationalism. On the other, the advocates of a cocktail of nationalism, racism, sexism, militarism, and authoritarianism that echoes the fascism of the 1930s.

The historical stakes are awesome. The challenge facing the Left, immense. We have to build big, broad, bold movements on every front – against their sexism, their racism, their nationalism, their warmongering, their climate-change denial – and we have to link those movements together and co-ordinate them internationally.

The Far Right is advancing arm-in-arm. It aims to pull apart the EU, to retreat into economic nationalism, to demonise the migrant and the Muslim, to unleash the police, to fill the prisons and the camps.

We must advance arm-in-arm. Against Brexit, Trump, and Le Pen. In defence of free movement. Against Islamophobia. For a united struggle from below to roll back racism and sexism, to defeat fascism, and to present a radical alternative to neoliberal capitalism and a vision of the world transformed.

# The parties of the Far Right in modern Europe

## BRITAIN

*Main far-right party:*[1] United Kingdom Independence Party (UKIP)

*% of vote:*[2] 12.6% (2015)

*What they stand for:*
– Regressive flat-rate income tax.
– Cutting 2 million public-sector jobs.
– Doubling prison places.
– Immigration freeze.
– Five-year qualification period for British citizenship.
– Doubling of defence expenditure.
– Privatisation of NHS.
– Cuts in benefits.
– Climate-change denial.

## FRANCE

*Main far-right parties:* National Front; Ligue du Sud

*% of vote:* National Front: 13.6% (2012); Ligue du Sud: n/a

*What they stand for:*
National Front:
– Respectable façade ('de-demonisation').
– Stripping dual nationality from 'extremists'.
– Public services prioritised for nationals.

– Le Pen prosecuted for comparing Muslims praying in public
to Nazi occupation.
– Children of undocumented parents to be denied free education.
– Net migration to be reduced to 10,000 per year.
– Increased minimum wage.
– Retirement age reduced to 60.
– Reduced energy prices and taxes
Ligue du Sud:
– Trade barriers to help small rather than big business.
– Links to Identitaires, an ethno-nationalist street movement.

## THE NETHERLANDS
*Main far-right party:* Party of Freedom
*% of vote:* 10.1% (2012)
*What they stand for:*
– Total 'de-Islamification' of the Netherlands.
– Blanket ban on migrants from Islamic countries.
– Ban on all Islamic symbols, mosques, and Koran.
– 'Welfare-chauvinism': social security to be dependent on
length of citizenship and language skills.
– Withdrawal from EU.
– Cutting all foreign aid.
– Boosting funding for police and security services.
– Banning of radical imams.
– Criminals with dual citizenship to be deported.
– Leader convicted of hate speech.

## BELGIUM
*Main far-right party:* Vlaams Belang
*% of vote:* 3.67% (2014)
*What they stand for:*
– Flemish independence.
– Repatriation of immigrants who 'reject, deny, or combat'
Flemish culture.

– Rejection of 'multicultural ideology'.
– Zero tolerance of crime.
– Small state.
– Low tax and low public spending.
– Pro-traditional family unit.

## DENMARK
*Main far-right party:* Danish Peoples Party
*% of vote:* 21.1% (2015)
*What they stand for:*
– Pro-National Church.
– Direct democracy.
– Being tough on crime.
– 'Denmark belongs to the Danes': very low immigration.
– Ending all non-Western immigration.
– Opposition to EU.
– Pro-traditional family unit.

## SWEDEN
*Main far-right party:* Sweden Democrats
*% of vote:* 12.9% (2014)
*What they stand for:*
– Raising unemployment benefits.
– Increasing number of hospital beds.
– More defence spending.
– Cutting taxes for pensioners.
– Increased child benefits.
– Closing borders to refugees from Syria and Iraq.
– Guaranteeing every young person a job.
– Smaller class sizes for 7 to 10-year-olds.
– Raising wages for teachers.
– Making Sweden free from fossil fuels by 2050.
– Pushing for tougher labour rights for all workers within EU.
– More serious punishments for sex offenders.

## GERMANY
*Main far-right party:* Alternative for Germany
*% of vote:* 4.7% (2013)
*What they stand for:*
– Conscription for 18-year-old men.
– Climate-change denial.
– Opposition to same-sex marriage or adoption.
– Against further EU integration.
– Support for Swiss-style direct democracy.
– Incompatibility of Islam with German constitution.
– Bans on minarets, call to prayer, burka, and niqab.
– Strict controls on migration.
– Hungarian-style border fence.
– Abolition of inheritance tax.
– Referendum on membership of euro.
– Links with far-right street movement Pegida.

## AUSTRIA
*Main far-right party:* Austrian Freedom Party
*% of vote:* 20.5% (2013)
*What they stand for:*
– Pro-Russia – signed co-operation agreement with Putin.
– Ban on Muslim symbols.
– Halving of asylum acceptances.
– Leader claims Islam threatens European society and Austria needs law which 'prohibits fascistic Islam'.

## SWITZERLAND
*Main far-right party:* Swiss People's Party
*% of vote:* 29.4% (2015)
*What they stand for:*
– Led campaign to stop building of minarets in 2009.
– Leader and deputy convicted of publishing racist election posters in 2015.

## ITALY
*Main far-right parties:* Northern League; National Alliance
*% of vote:* Northern League 4.08% (2013); National Alliance 1.95% (2013)
*What they stand for:*
Northern League:
– No euro.
– End to mass immigration.
– Single flat tax-rate of 15%.
– Links to fascist street movement Casa Pound.
– Co-organised 25,000-strong far-right march in Rome in 2015.
– Leader has called for Roma camps to be razed.
National Alliance:
– Claims Muslims 'trying to impose a way of life that is incompatible with ours'.
– Eurosceptic.
– Neoliberal.
– Co-organised 25,000-strong far-right march in Rome in 2015.

## SLOVAKIA
*Main far-right parties:* Slovak National Party; Kotleba – People's Party Our Slovakia
*% of vote:* Slovak National Party 8.6%; Kotleba – People's Party Our Slovakia 8%
*What they stand for:*
Slovak National Party:
– Anti-Hungarian and anti-Roma racism.
– Former leader said 'Hungarians are a cancer in the body of the Slovak nation' and Roma should be dealt with using 'a long whip in a small yard'.
Kotleba – People's Party Our Slovakia:
– Wants 'home guard' to stop 'gypsy extremists' who 'steal, rape, and murder'.

## CZECH REPUBLIC
*Main far-right party:* Dawn – National Coalition
*% of vote:* 6.88% (2013)
*What they stand for:*
– Opposition to immigration.
– Direct democracy.
– Links to far-right street movement.

## HUNGARY
*Main far-right parties:* Fidesz; Jobbik
*% of vote:* Fidesz 44.8% (2014); Jobbik 21% (2014)
*What they stand for:*
Fidesz:
– Sacked state employees opposed to government.
– Heavily amended constitution to give executive more power.
– Gerrymandered voting system.
– Gave citizenship to every ethnic Hungarian around the world.
– Opposed to mass immigration.
– Requires public media journalists to promote national identity.
– Irredentist policy towards parts of Slovakia, Romania, and Serbia.
Jobbik:
– Hard line on crime.
– Racialisation of crime.
– Links to far-right paramilitaries.
– Refers to 'gypsy crime' and says 'Hungary belongs to Hungarians'.

## BULGARIA
*Main far-right parties:* Ataka; Patriotic Front
*% of vote:* Ataka 4.52% (2014); Patriotic Front 7.3% (2014)
*What they stand for:*
Ataka:
– Founder and chairman has authored several books on 'global Jewish conspiracy'.

- Demands mono-ethnic Bulgaria.
- Withdrawal from NATO.
- Renegotiation of EU accession treaty.
- Breaking relations with IMF and World Bank.
- Ban on Turkish-language TV programmes.
- Slogans include 'Condemn gypsies to work camps!', 'All Roma are criminals', and 'Homosexuals are sick'.
- Pro-Orthodox Christian.

Patriotic Front:
- National economic revival.
- Modernisation of healthcare and education.
- Fighting corruption.

## GREECE
*Main far-right party:* Golden Dawn
*% of vote:* 7% (2015)
*What they stand for:*
- Irredentist policy towards various Turkish regions.
- Racial supremacy of Greeks.
- Zero tolerance of immigration.
- Rejection of representative democracy.
- Use of violent paramilitaries ('battalion squads').

## POLAND
*Main far-right parties:* Law and Justice Party; Kukiz'15; Korwin
*% of vote:* Law and Justice Party 37.58% (2015); Kukiz'15 8.81% (2015); Korwin 4.7% (2015)
*What they stand for:*
Law and Justice Party:
- Ban on abortion and IVF treatment.
- Opposition to immigration.
- Family-focused welfare spending.
- Soft Euroscepticism.
- Support for Catholic Church.

– Further taxes on banks and supermarkets to pay for benefits for pensioners and workers.
Kukiz'15:
– Prioritising local companies over foreign ones.

## UKRAINE
*Main far-right parties:* Svoboda; Pravy Sektor
*% of vote:* Svoboda 4.71% (2014); Pravy Sektor 1.8% (2014)
*What they stand for:*
Svoboda:
– Ukrainian nationalist and anti-Russian/anti-Communist.
– Opposition to abortion and LGBT rights.
– Anti-semitism.
Pravy Sektor:
– Militant nationalism.
– Paramilitary organisation.
– Involved in fighting in Eastern Ukraine.

## RUSSIA
*Main far-right party:* United Russia
*% of vote:* 54.2% (2016)
*What they stand for:*
– Cult of personality around Putin.
– Increased military spending.
– Increased public spending (initially).
– Brutal crackdowns on Chechens.
– Passed anti-LGBT laws.
– Massive repression of protest.
– Accused of vote rigging.
– Suppression of free press and assassination of reporters.
– Annexed Crimea.

## TURKEY
*Main far-right party:* Justice and Development Party
*% of vote:* 49.5% (2015)
*What they stand for:*
– Conservative Islamist.
– Purging of opponents in state.
– Amended constitution to grant executive more power.
– Increased public spending (initially).
– Repression of protest.
– Heavy repression and rights abuses against Kurds.

# Bibliography

For each reference work cited, I give both the date of first publication and that of the edition I used.

Behan, T, 2003, *The Resistable Rise of Benito Mussolini*, London, Bookmarks.

Calder, A, 1969/1992, *The People's War: Britain, 1939-1945*, London, Pimlico.

Callinicos, A, 2016, 'The end of the world news', in *International Socialism* 153, at www.isj.org.uk

Caplan, J, 2016, 'Trump and Fascism: a view from the past', *History Workshop*, www.historyworkshop.org.uk

Chaudhary, A J and Chappe, Raphaële, 2016, 'The Supermanagerial Reich', in *Los Angeles Review of Books*, 7/11/16.

*Commission Nationale Anti-Fasciste, NPA*, 'France: Pétain's children' in F Leplat (ed.), *The Far Right in Europe*, London, Resistance Books, 113-201.

Cousins, A, 2011, 'The Crisis of the British Regime: democracy, protest, and the unions, at www.countefire.org

El-Gingihy, Y, 2015, *How to Dismantle the NHS in 10 Easy Steps*, Winchester, Zero Books.

Fabry, A, 2015, 'The Far Right in Hungary', in F Leplat (ed.), *The Far Right in Europe*, London, Resistance Books, 202-47.

Faulkner, N, 2013a, *A Marxist History of the World*, London, Pluto.

Faulkner, N, 2013b, *No Glory: the real history of the First World War*, London, Stop the War Coalition.

Faulkner, N, 2016a, *Boom, Bubble, and Bust: an activist guide to the capitalist crisis and the radical alternative*, London, Brick Lane Debates Corbynomics Group.

Faulkner, N, 2016b, 'Corbynomics Can Work', in *Red Pepper*, 207, 18-21.

Faulkner, N, 2016c, 'Debt and Democracy: an existential crisis', in *Agora*, 1, 24-27.

Faulkner, N, 2017, *A People's History of the Russian Revolution*, London, Pluto/Left Book Club.

Fest, J C, 1973/1987, *Hitler*, London, Weidenfeld and Nicolson.

Fromm, E, 1941, *Escape From Freedom* (aka *The Fear of Freedom*), New York, Farrar & Rinehart.

Galbraith, J K, 1958/1970, *The Affluent Society*, Harmondsworth, Penguin.

Gardiner, J, 2010/2011, *The Thirties: an intimate history*, London, Harper.

Goodwin, M and Heath, O, 2016, 'Brexit vote explained: poverty, low skills, and lack of opportunities', Joseph Rowntree Foundation, www.jrf.org.uk

Grunberger, R, 1971/1974, *A Social History of the Third Reich*, London, Penguin.

Hearse, P, 2015, 'UKIP and the politics of ultra-Thatcherism', in F Leplat (ed.), *The Far Right in Europe*, London, Resistance Books, 34-63.

Hobsbawm, E, 1987/1994, *The Age of Empire, 1875-1914*, London, Abacus.

Jacobs, J, 1978/1991, *Out of the Ghetto*, London, Phoenix.

Jong, A de, 2015, 'National-populism in the Netherlands', in F Leplat (ed.), *The Far Right in Europe*, London, Resistance Books, 266-310.

Kershaw, I, 1998/1999, *Hitler, 1889-1936: hubris*, London, Penguin.

Kershaw, I, 2000/2001, *Hitler, 1936-1945: nemesis*, London, Penguin.

Kershaw, I, 2011, *The End: Hitler's Germany, 1944-45*, London,

Penguin.

Klein, N, 2016, 'Trump's crony cabinet may look strong, but they are scared', in *The Nation*, 26/1/2017.

Lister, R, 1996, 'Forward', in C Murray et al, *Charles Murray and the Underclass: the developing debate*, London, IEA Health and Welfare Unit.

Mack Smith, D, 1993/1994, *Mussolini*, London, Phoenix.

Mair, P, 2013, *Ruling the Void: the hollowing of Western democracy*, London, Verso.

Marx, K, 1852/1973, 'The Eighteenth Brumaire of Louis Bonaparte', in D Fernbach (ed.), *Surveys from Exile*, Harmondsworth, Penguin.

Noakes, J and Pridham, G (eds.), 1983, *Nazism, 1919-1934, Vol. 1, The Rise to Power*, Exeter, University of Exeter.

Noakes, J and Pridham, G (eds.), 1984, *Nazism, 1919-1945, Vol. 2, State, Economy, and Society, 1933-1939*, Exeter, University of Exeter.

Orwell, G, 1938/1966, *Homage to Catalonia*, Harmondsworth, Penguin.

Paxton, R, 2004, *The Anatomy of Fascism*, London, Allen Lane.

Piketty, T, 2013/2014, *Capital in the 21st Century*, Cambridge, Massachusetts, Harvard.

Piratin, P, 1948/1978, *Our Flag Stays Red*, London, Lawrence and Wishart.

Reich, W, 1933/1975, *The Mass Psychology of Fascism*, Harmondsworth, Penguin.

Renton, D, 2006, *When We Touched the Sky: the Anti-Nazi League, 1977-1981*, Cheltenham, New Clarion Press.

Skidelsky, R, 1975, *Oswald Mosley*, New York, Holt, Rinehart, and Winston.

Sparks, C, 1980, *Never Again! The hows and whys of stopping fascism*, London, Bookmarks.

Thomas, H, 1961/1986, *The Spanish Civil War*, Harmondsworth, Penguin.

Trotsky, L, 1931a/1971, 'For a workers' united front against fascism', in *The Struggle Against Fascism in Germany*, New York, Pathfinder, 152-63.

Trotsky, L, 1931b/1971, 'Germany: the key to the international situation', in *The Struggle Against Fascism in Germany*, New York, Pathfinder, 133-51.

Trotsky, L, 1932a/1971, 'The German puzzle', in *The Struggle Against Fascism in Germany*, New York, Pathfinder, 305-12.

Trotsky, L, 1932b/1971, 'What next?', in *The Struggle Against Fascism in Germany*, New York, Pathfinder, 164-297.

Trotsky, 1933/1971, 'The united front for defence', in *The Struggle Against Fascism in Germany*, New York, Pathfinder, 404-27.

Trotsky, L, 1934/1971, 'Bonapartism and fascism', in *The Struggle Against Fascism in Germany*, New York, Pathfinder, 509-16.

Trotsky, L, 1973, *The Spanish Revolution (1931-39)*, New York, Pathfinder.

Turner, A, 2016, *Between Debt and the Devil: money, credit, and fixing global finance*, Princeton, Princeton University Press.

United States Census Bureau, 2016, *Income, Poverty, and Health Insurance Coverage in the United States: 2015*, www.census.gov

Wade, W C, 1987/1988, *The Fiery Cross: the Ku Klux Klan in America*, New York, Touchstone/Simon & Schuster.

Walker, M, 1977, *The National Front*, Glasgow, Fontana.

Widgery, D, 1986, *Beating Time*, London, Chatto & Windus.

Wilkinson, R and Pickett, K, 2009/2010, *The Spirit Level: why equality is better for everyone*, London, Penguin.

Woodward, J, 2017, 'It's China, stupid: Trump and US foreign policy', at www.newcoldwar.typepad.com/blog

# Notes

## INTRODUCTION

1. The usual caveat applies: the appearance of their names here does not imply agreement with any particular statement in the text.
2. This is to compare Tory Prime Minister Theresa May's fawning on Trump with the policy of her interwar predecessor, Neville Chamberlain, whose 'appeasement' of Hitler eased his progress to European hegemony before the outbreak of the Second World War.

## CHAPTER 1

1. *Independent*, 'Former KKK leader David Duke: "We won it for Donald Trump."', 9/11/16.
2. Caplan 2016.
3. *Independent*, 'Farage says UK can "do business" with Trump after becoming first British politician to meet President-elect', 12/11/16.
4. *Independent*, 'Boris Johnson carries out screeching U-turn on Donald Trump', 9/11/16.
5. *Daily Telegraph*, 'Theresa May says Donald Trump's victory shows Britain needs to control immigration', 14/11/16.
6. Source: Goodwin and Heath 2016.
7. Goodwin and Heath 2016.
8. Trotsky 1925/26, 'The Programme of Peace', www.marxists.org. We are grateful to Liam Mac Uaid and Socialist

Democracy (www.socialistdemocracy.org) for drawing our attention to this reference.

9. *Guardian*, 'Labour is in his sights but May should worry too', 29/11/16.
10. www.rt.com/news/367284-austria-elections-trump-hofer
11. www.independent.co.uk/voices/italy-referendum-matteo-renzi-trump-effect
12. *Guardian*, 'Far-right leader found guilty of insulting Dutch Moroccans in televised speech', 10/12/16.
13. www.independent.co.uk/news/world/europe/donald-trump-geert-wilders-president-win-response-patriotic-spring-europe-revolution-take-country
14. www.rt.com/news/367210-france-elections-putin-trump-peace
15. www.humanite.fr/beziers-la-creation-de-la-milice-de-robert-menard-suspendue-par-la-justice
16. www.theguardian.com/world/2016/nov/27/francois-fillon-on-course-to-win-french-primary-to-be-candidate-for-the-right

## CHAPTER 2
1. Paxton 2004, 8, 23.
2. Trotsky 1934/1971, 515-6.
3. Thomas 1961/1986, 506, 508; Faulkner 2013a, 235-8.
4. Paxton 2004, 23.
5. Faulkner 2013a, 221-38.
6. Orwell 1938/1966, 8-10.
7. www.getty.edu/art/exhibitions/heartfield
8. Wade 1987/1988, 269, 273.
9. Mack Smith 1993/1994, 51; Behan 2003, 41.
10. Sparks 1980, 32-3; Kershaw 1998/1999, 190.
11. Skidelsky 1975, 322-3.
12. Kershaw 1998/1999, 413.
13. Trotsky 1931a/1971, 163.
14. Sparks 1980, 38-9; Faulkner 2013a, 239-40.

15. Sparks 1980, 38.
16. Sparks 1980, 38.
17. Skidelsky 1975, 226-8.
18. Faulkner 2013a, 239-40.
19. Trotsky 1933/1971, 420.
20. Trotsky 1932a/1971, 308.
21. Trotsky 1932b/1971, 179-80.
22. Sparks 1980, 31.
23. www.independent.co.uk/news/uk/home-news/britain-now-has-7-social-classes-and-working-class-is-a-dwindling-breed
24. Marx 1852/1973, 197.
25. Lister 1996, 5-6.
26. Goodwin and Heath 2016.
27. For example, Trotsky 1931b/1971, 148.
28. Hobsbawm's trilogy of books on the period, *The Age of Revolution (1789-1848)*, *The Age of Capital (1848-1875)*, and *The Age of Empire (1875-1914)*, are seminal works.
29. Two studies, *Nations and Nationalism since 1780* and *The Invention of Tradition*, are of particular importance. We should add this point. Nationalism can provide the ideological framework for mass mobilisation of the oppressed against their oppressors, whether in the form of revolts against foreign rule or revolts by oppressed minorities within the nation-state. The Irish War of Independence (1919-21) is an example of the former. The 'Troubles' in Northern Ireland (1969-98) is an example of the latter. In all such cases, socialists should support the struggles of the oppressed, even when waged in a nationalist framework. We are not concerned with this form of nationalism anywhere in this book, however, and nothing more will be said about it. Our focus is exclusively on the nationalism of the *oppressor* – that is, of imperial powers and right-wing forces.
30. Faulkner 2013b, 7.
31. These extracts are taken from translations of Mussolini's

speeches concerning Ethiopia in 1935 that can be found online.

32. Renton 2006, 22.
33. See Wyn Craig Wade's *The Fiery Cross: the Ku Klux Klan in America* for a detailed narrative history.
34. Wade 1987/1988, 31-79 *passim*.
35. The Black Hundreds were semi-official paramilitaries used in anti-semitic pogroms and attacks on the working-class movement in the years before the Russian Revolution. The *Freikorps* were right-wing paramilitaries formed of demobilised servicemen, especially junior officers and NCOs, who were used against the Left during the German Revolution of 1918-23. The Blackshirts were the paramilitary arm of the Italian National Fascist Party from 1919 until the fall of the Mussolini regime in 1943.
36. Wade 1987/1988, 119-247 *passim*.
37. Wade 1987/1988, 276-367 *passim*.
38. Noakes and Pridham 1984, 449.
39. The Cleansing of the Augean Stables was one of the Labours of Herakles. It involved washing away a vast accumulation of cattle dung.
40. Trotsky 1932a/1971, 308.
41. The Enlightenment was a broad intellectual movement of the late 17th to early 19th century which challenged the ideology of the absolutist state, the Catholic Church, and traditional feudal elites, and counter-posed the claims of reason, intellect, and scientific enquiry. In an intellectual sense, fascism represents regression to a pre-scientific, and therefore pre-Enlightenment, way of thinking. Climate-change denial is an obvious example.
42. Wade 1987/1988, 203-4. The author of the piece was named Nguyen Sinh Cung. He later returned to Vietnam and changed his name to Ho Chi Minh.
43. The 'return of the repressed' is a key psychoanalytical concept. Desires that the social order cannot accommo-

date are repressed and driven into the unconscious part of the human mind. They nonetheless remain potent and in search of an outlet. They resurface in disguised and distorted forms – in neurotic symptoms for example – and sometimes in destructive, psychotic form, when rage and violence may predominate.

44. His key study was *The Mass Psychology of Fascism* (1933). Reich's work became increasingly eccentric and questionable, but this should not be allowed to detract from the significance of his theoretical contributions in the interwar period.
45. Reich 1933/1975, 17.
46. Reich 1933/1975, 137.
47. His key study was *Fear of Freedom* (1941).
48. Reich 1933/1975, 362.
49. Reich 1933/1975, 362.
50. Reich 1933/1975, 199.
51. Reich 1933/1975, 375-6.

**CHAPTER 3**
1. Hitler, Vol 2, Chpt 6, www.mondopolitico.com/library/meinkampf
2. Wade 1987/1988, 255.
3. Walker 1977, 145.
4. Walker 1977, 184.
5. These were London's three largest venues at the time.
6. Skidelsky 1975, 365, 336.
7. Wade 1987/1988, 216, 185.
8. Fest 1973/1987, 238.
9. Skidelsky 1975, 312.
10. Behan 2003, 44-50; Paxton 2004, 58-64.
11. Sparks 1980, 51-62.
12. These are rough estimates: there is much dispute about the figures.
13. Thomas 1961/1986, 506.

14. Skidelsky 1975, 367-78.
15. Wade 1987/1988, 79.
16. Wade 1987/1988, 164.
17. Wade 1987/1988, 164-5, 171, 183.
18. Wade 1987/1988, 195.
19. Wade 1987/1988, 368-71.
20. We capitalise 'Fascist' when referring specifically to the Italian movement of that name.
21. Paxton 2004, 88-90.
22. Paxton 2004, 120, 122, 124.
23. Mack Smith 1993/1994, 56-151 *passim*.
24. Paxton 2004, 91-6, 119-21.
25. Paxton 2004, 147.
26. Kershaw 1998/1999, 431-68 *passim*.
27. Kershaw 2011, 400.
28. Noakes and Pridham 1983, 14-6.
29. Grunberger 1971/1974, 82-3.
30. Kershaw 1998/1999, 473-5, 560-73; 2000/2001, 130-6.
31. Kershaw 1998/1999, 512-22.

## CHAPTER 4

1. Much of the material in this section has appeared elsewhere. See Faulkner 2016a, 2016b, and 2016c. Special thanks are due to Brick Lane Debates, *Red Pepper*, and *Agora*.
2. These circuits can be expressed as follows: the industrial circuit is M – C – M+, where M is the money invested, C is the commodities consumed in production (raw materials, energy, machinery, labour-power), and M+ is the money recouped with a profit; whereas the financial circuit is M – (M) – M+, where M is the money invested, (M) is a monetary asset/paper title, and M+ is the money recouped with a profit.
3. *Guardian*, 'Let's talk about debts', 12/1/2017.
4. El-Gingihy 2015, 9-10.
5. *Guardian*, 'Battered by crises and short of ideas, Union is in

retreat', 6/1/2017.

6. Faulkner 2016a, 10.
7. *Fortune*, 'Top CEOs make more than 300 times the average worker', 22/6/2015.
8. Piketty 2013/2014, 332.
9. Piketty 2013/2014, 281.
10. Piketty 2013/2014, 171.
11. United States Census Bureau 2016.
12. *Guardian*, 'How Trump took Middletown', 16/11/2016.
13. Goodwin and Heath 2016.
14. Wilkinson and Pickett 2009/2010, *passim*.
15. Hobsbawm's *The Age of Empire* (1987/1994) is the key study.
16. Calder 1969/1992.
17. Faulkner 2013a, 186.
18. Gardiner 2010/2011, 379-83.
19. Calder 1969/1992, 163-227 *passim*.
20. Source: *British Social Attitudes 30*, www.bsa.natcen.ac.uk
21. Source: *Eurobarometer*, www.ec.europa.eu
22. Source: Gallup, www.gallup.com
23. Sources: Mair 2013, 17-44 *passim*; International IDEA, www.idea.int; UK Political Info, www.ukpolitical.info
24. Sources: Gallup, www.gallup.com; Pew Research Centre, www.assets.pewresearch.org
25. Mair 2013, 1.
26. Mair 2013, 82-3.
27. Mair 2013, 84-5.
28. Mair 2013, 90-8.

**CHAPTER 5**
1. This chapter in particular is heavily dependent on online research carried out by Samir Dathi.
2. Hearse 2015, 49-50.
3. *Commission Nationale Anti-Fasciste, NPA*, 125.
4. Jong 2015, *passim*.
5. *Guardian*, 'Europe: "He is showing how it's done" – ban is

backed by rightwing politicians', 31/1/2017.

6. *Commission Nationale Anti-Fasciste, NPA*, 151n.
7. *Commission Nationale Anti-Fasciste, NPA*, 152-3.
8. *Guardian*, 'Trump's war on Islam', 31/1/2017.
9. The Nuremburg Laws of 1935 deprived Jews of their German citizenship and its associated rights and protections, and made it illegal for them to intermarry with Gentiles. The nationwide anti-Jewish pogrom in Nazi Germany on the night of 9/10 November became known as *Kristallnacht*, the 'night of broken glass', because of the smashed windows.
10. *Guardian*, 'Suddenly, Muslims are America's pariahs', 30/1/2017.
11. Marienna Pope-Weidemann, 'If we win the fight to let refugees into Fortress Britain, the world will take note', *Guardian*, 29/12/2016.
12. *Guardian*, 'The ideologically driven group behind policy', 30/1/2017.
13. Callinicos 2016.
14. Callinicos 2016.
15. Hearse 2015, 53-4.
16. Fabry 2015, 222-8.
17. Recent repetition of this Holocaust denial lead to his expulsion by his own daughter from the party he founded!
18. *Guardian*, 'Can this man make Marine Le Pen president', 31/1/2017.
19. *Guardian*, 'Four more journalists get felony charges after covering inauguration unrest', 24/1/2017.
20. *Guardian*, 'Anti-pipeline activists and film-makers face prison, raising fears for free press', 30/1/2017.
21. *Independent*, 'The acting attorney general was fired for defying Trump. Here's the message she left for lawyers', 31/1/2017.

## CHAPTER 6
1. These can be found at www.youtube.com/watch?v=2hLYavpMSFs and www.youtube.com/watch?v=opn15-59L1I
2. Sparks 1980, 58.
3. Trotsky 1931a, 163.
4. Cousins 2011, esp. Graph 22.
5. Skidelsky 1975, 257.
6. The history of the BUF is covered in detail in Skidelsky 1975, in summary form in Sparks 1980, and realistically enough in the 1998 Channel 4 mini-series *Mosley*.
7. *Commission Nationale Anti-Fasciste, NPA* 2015, 153-8.
8. *Commission Nationale Anti-Fasciste, NPA* 2015, 167.
9. *Guardian*, 'The heavens wept and so should we for broken democracy', 21/1/17.
10. Chaudary and Chappe 2016.
11. *Salon*, 'Donald Trump's "inverted totalitarianism": too bad we didn't heed Sheldon Wolin's warnings', 23/11/16.
12. *Huffington Post*, 'Trump vows immediate action against "anti-police atmosphere" in US', 20/1/17.

## CHAPTER 7
1. Sparks 1980, 55.
2. A summary of the role of the KPD in the events in Germany can be found in Sparks 1980, 51-62. Trotsky's main writings on the subject are included in *The Struggle Against Fascism in Germany* (Pathfinder, 1971); they can also be accessed at www.marxists.org
3. See Faulkner 2017, 208-50, for an analysis of this process.
4. A summary of the role of the PCE in the events in Spain can be found in Sparks 1980, 63-71. Trotsky's main writings on the subject are included in *The Spanish Revolution, 1931-39* (Pathfinder, 1973); they can also be accessed at www.marxists.org
5. Two good accounts of the Battle of Cable Street can be found in Piratin 1948/1978 and Jacobs 1978/1991 – the former

giving the perspective of a CP loyalist, the latter that of an East End dissident.

6. Piratin 1948/1978, 20.
7. Piratin 1948/1978, 23-4.
8. Gardiner 2010/2011, 152-81.
9. Sparks 1980, 78-9.
10. Renton 2006, 1-31; Widgery 1986, 17.
11. The IS/SWP was a very different organisation in the 1970s (and 1980s) from the small, self-perpetuating, self-referencing sect it has degenerated into today. It was a magnet for young activists, many of them quite anarchic, and its whole ethos was to encourage bottom-up democracy, spontaneity, and self-activity.
12. Renton 2006, 52-50; Widgery 1986 *passim*.
13. Renton 2006, 51-73.
14. Renton 2006, 72.
15. Widgery 1986, 48-9.
16. Renton 2006, 175-80.
17. *Daily Telegraph*, 'Theresa May's Brexit speech in full', 17/1/2017.
18. *Guardian*, 'Corbyn stance on EU immigration "risks helping UKIP"', 8/12/2016.
19. *Guardian*, 'Andy Burnham: Labour wrong to put single market ahead of immigration', 16/12/2016.
20. *Independent*, 'Corbyn's Momentum group launches nationwide campaign to "take back control" of Brexit', 25/11/2016.
21. We are bound to critique arguments with which we disagree, especially arguments we consider so profoundly dangerous because they disorient and disarm activists in the face of the fascist menace. But we wish to avoid personalising the argument, so we are not giving a reference here.
22. Renton 2006, 170.
23. Renton 2006, 171.

## CONCLUSION
1. www.versobooks.com/blogs/1683-ten-theses-on-the-far-right-in-europe-by-michael-lowy
2. cf Löwy Thesis IV.
3. cf Löwy Theses III and V.
4. cf Löwy Theses VIII and IX.
5. cf Löwy Thesis I.
6. cf Löwy Thesis VI.
7. Woodward 2017.
8. cf Löwy Theses I and VII.
9. cf Löwy Thesis X.

## POSTSCRIPT
1. Klein 2017.
2. edition.cnn.com/2017/01/27/politics/trump-march-for-life-call
3. This section compiled from online data by Samir Dathi.
4. This section complied from online data by Andrew Burgin.

## APPENDIX
1. We include all parties of the Far Right in a single category, since all are in flux and are capable of evolving into more racist and violent forms of fascism.
2. We have given the figures for the most recent national-election results available at the time of writing.

# Index

Only substantive references are listed.